Stories for a Faithful Heart

OTHER BOOKS COMPILED BY ALICE GRAY

Stories for the Heart

More Stories for the Heart

Christmas Stories for the Heart

Stories for the Family's Heart

Stories for a Woman's Heart

Stories for a Man's Heart

Stories for a Teen's Heart

Keepsakes for the Heart—Mothers

Keepsakes for the Heart—Friendship

Keepsakes for the Heart—Love

Keepsakes for the Heart—Faith

Stories for a faithful Heart

This Billy Graham Evangelistic Association
special edition is published with permission
from Multnomah Publishers.

Over 100 Treasures for Your Soul

COMPILED BY ALICE GRAY

Multnomah® Publishers *Sisters, Oregon*

*We have done our best to diligently seek reprint permission and provide accurate source attribution for
all selections used in this book. However, if any attribution be found to be incorrect or lacking the
proper permission license, the publisher welcomes notification and written documentation supporting
corrections for subsequent printings. If you are, or know of the proper copyright holder for any such story
in this book, please contact us and we will properly credit and reimburse the contributor. We gratefully
acknowledge the cooperation of other publishers and individuals for granting permission to use their material
in this book. Please see the bibliography at the back of the book for complete attributions for this material.*

STORIES FOR THE FAITHFUL HEART
published by Multnomah Publishers, Inc.
© 2000 by Alice Gray

Design by Stephen Gardner / Cover illustration by Superstock

Scripture quotations are from:
The Holy Bible, New International Version (NIV)
© 1973, 1984 by International Bible Society,
used by permission of Zondervan Publishing House
Also quoted:
The Message © 1993 by Eugene H. Peterson
The Holy Bible, New King James Version (NKJV) © 1984 by Thomas Nelson, Inc.
The Living Bible (TLB) © 1971. Used by permission of Tyndale House Publishers, Inc.
All rights reserved.
The Holy Bible, King James Version (KJV)
Multnomah is a trademark of Multnomah Publishers, Inc.,
and is registered in the U.S. Patent and Trademark Office.
The colophon is a trademark of Multnomah Publishers, Inc.
Printed in the United States of America

For information:
MULTNOMAH PUBLISHERS, INC.
POST OFFICE BOX 1720
SISTERS, OREGON 97759
Library of Congress Cataloging-in-Publication Data:

Stories for a faithful heart: over 100 treasures to touch your soul / compiled by Alice Gray.

ISBN 0-913367-17-6
        1. Christian life. I. Gray, Alice, 1939-

To the women who attended *Joy in the Morning*—
Our lives were changed.

JOY IN THE MORNING

Joy in the morning,

Joy in the day,

Joy through the trials,

Joy on the way.

Weeping may last for the nighttime,

But in the morning comes joy.

PATTI BISENIUS
ADAPTED FROM PSALM 30:5

A Special Thank You to:

Teri Sharp
For eleventh hour help and encouragement

Jennifer Gates
For endless hours of research

Penny Whipps
For an understanding heart

Doreen Button, Casandra Lindell, and Ruth King
For helping me choose tender and uplifting stories

Readers from around the world who submitted stories,
I was deeply touched by your words.
I wish we could have used all your stories.

Brandy Gilmore and Rachel Neet
For long days and midnight hours in preparing the manuscript

Al Gray
For tenderly caring for me
I love it when you encourage me to take a break and
we walk holding hands, and are so glad to be together.

CONTENTS

Making a Difference

Changed Lives

Because I Care

Compassion

KINDNESS

I have wept in the night for the shortness of sight
That to somebody's need made me blind;
But I never have yet felt a tinge of regret
For being a little too kind.

AUTHOR UNKNOWN
FROM *IN THE COMPANY OF FRIENDS*

LAVENDER MEMORIES

SANDRA PICKLESIMER ALDRICH AND BOBBIE VALENTINE
FROM *HEARTPRINTS*

s Cotha Prior strolled past the new shop that sold body lotions and soaps, the lavender-wrapped bars displayed in the window caught her attention. Her daughter, Monica, would like those. Once inside, Cotha picked up the closest bar and held it to her nose. The fragrance carried her back to her childhood.

She remembered Margie, the little girl in her fifth grade class who always was poorly dressed and whose bathing habits were, well, not one of her regular habits. Even at that young age, Cotha knew how important the opinions of her friends were, so although she felt sorry for Margie, she couldn't risk being friends with her.

Then one afternoon, as the young Cotha colored the states on her homework worksheet, she casually mentioned Margie to her mother, who stopped in the middle of stirring the stew to ask, "What's her family like?"

Cotha didn't look up. "Oh, really poor, I guess," she answered.

"Well, it sounds as though she needs a friend," Mrs. Burnett said. "Why don't you invite her to spend Friday night with you?"

Cotha looked up quickly then. "You mean *here?* Spend the night with me? But, Mom, she *smells.*"

"Cotha Helen." Her mother's use of both names meant the situation was settled. There was nothing to do but invite Margie home. The next morning Cotha hesitantly whispered the invitation at the end of recess while her friends were hanging up their jackets and combing their hair. Margie looked suspicious, so Cotha added, "My mother said it's okay. Here's a note from my mother to give to yours."

So two days later they rode the school bus home while Cotha tried to ignore the surprised looks on her friends' faces as they saw the two of them together. Have two fifth grade girls ever been quieter? Cotha thought of other times when she'd been invited to spend the night with a friend. They would talk and giggle all the way to their stop.

Finally Cotha gave a determined little huff and said to Margie, "I've got a cat. She's going to have kittens."

Margie's eyes lit up. "Oh, I like cats." Then she frowned as though recalling a painful memory and added, "But my dad doesn't."

Cotha didn't know what to say then, so she feigned interest in something outside the school bus window.

Both girls were silent until the bus rolled to a stop in front of the white house with the green shutters.

Mrs. Burnett was in the kitchen. She greeted Cotha and Margie warmly and then gestured toward the table set with two glasses of milk and banana bread. "Why don't you girls have a little snack while I tend to dinner," she said.

When the banana bread was finished, Mrs. Burnett handed each child identical paper-doll books and blunted scissors. Dressing the paper women in shiny dresses gave them something in common to talk about. By the time they washed their hands for dinner, they were chatting enthusiastically about school.

After the dishes were done, Mrs. Burnett said, "Time to take a bath before bed, girls." Then she held out scented soaps wrapped in lavender paper. "Since this is a special night, I thought you might like to use fancy soaps," she said. "Cotha, you first, and I'll wash your back for you."

Then it was Margie's turn. If she was nervous about having an adult bathe her, she didn't show it. As the tub filled, Mrs. Burnett poured in a double capful of her own guarded bubble bath. "Don't you just love bubble baths, Margie?" she asked as though the child bathed in such luxury every day.

She turned to pull Margie's grimy dress over her head, then said, "I'll look away as you take the other things off, but be careful climbing into the tub. That brand of bubble bath makes it slippery."

Once Margie was settled into the warm water, Mrs. Burnett knelt down and soaped the wet washcloth heavily before rubbing it over the child's back.

"Oh, that feels good," was all Margie said.

Mrs. Burnett chatted about how quickly Cotha and Margie were growing and what lovely young women they were already. Repeatedly she soaped the washcloth and scrubbed Margie's gray skin until it shone pink.

Through the whole thing Cotha was thinking, *Oh, how can she do that? Margie is so dirty.* But Mrs. Burnett continued to scrub cheerfully, then washed Margie's hair several times. Once Margie was out of the tub, Mrs. Burnett dried her back and dusted her thin shoulders with scented talcum. Then, since Margie had brought no nightclothes, Mrs. Burnett pulled one of Cotha's clean nightgowns over Margie's now shining head.

After tucking both girls under quilts, Mrs. Burnett leaned over to gently kiss them good night. Margie beamed. As Mrs. Burnett whispered, "Good night, girls," and turned out the light, Margie pulled the clean sheets to her nose and breathed deeply. Then she fell asleep almost immediately.

Cotha was amazed that her new friend fell asleep so quickly; she was used to talking and giggling for a long time with her other friends. To the sound of Margie's gentle breathing, Cotha stared at the shadows on the wall, thinking about all her mother had done. During Margie's bath, Mrs. Burnett had never once said anything to embarrass the girl, and she'd never even commented about how grimy the tub was afterward. She just scrubbed it out, quietly humming the whole time. Somehow Cotha knew her mother had washed more than Margie's dingy skin.

All these years later, the adult Cotha stood in the fragrant store, the lavender soap still in her hand, wondering where Margie was now. Margie had never mentioned Cotha's mother's ministrations, but Cotha had noticed a difference in the girl. Not only did Margie start coming to school clean and pleasant on the outside, but she had an inside sparkle that came, perhaps, from knowing someone cared. For the rest of the school year, Cotha and Margie played at recess and ate lunch together. When Margie's family moved at the end of the school year, Cotha never heard from her again, but she knew they had both been influenced by her mother's behavior.

Cotha smiled, then picked up a second bar of the lavender soap. She'd send that one to her mother, with a letter saying that she remembered what her mom had done all those years ago—not only for Margie but for Cotha as well.

Blessed are the merciful, for they will be shown mercy.

MATTHEW 5:7

PÃO, SENHOR?

MAX LUCADO
FROM *NO WONDER THEY CALL HIM THE SAVIOR*

He couldn't have been over six years old. Dirty face, barefeet, torn T-shirt, matted hair. He wasn't too different from the other hundred thousand or so street orphans that roam Rio de Janeiro.

I was walking to get a cup of coffee at a nearby café when he came up behind me. With my thoughts between the task I had just finished and the class I was about to teach, I scarcely felt the tap, tap, tap on my hand. I stopped and turned. Seeing no one, I continued on my way. I'd only taken a few steps, however, when I felt another insistent tap, tap, tap. This time I stopped and looked downward. There he stood. His eyes were whiter because of his grubby cheeks and coal-black hair.

"Pão, Senhor?" ("Bread, sir?")

Living in Brazil, one has daily opportunities to buy a candy bar or sandwich for these little outcasts. It's the least one can do. I told him to come with me and we entered the sidewalk café. "Coffee for me and something tasty for my little friend." The boy ran to the pastry counter and made his choice. Normally, these youngsters take food and scamper back out into the street without a word. But this little fellow surprised me.

The café consisted of a long bar: one end for pastries and the other for coffee. As the boy was making his choice, I went to the other end of the bar and began drinking my coffee. Just as I was getting my derailed train of thought back on track, I saw him again. He was standing in the café entrance, on tiptoe, bread in hand, looking in at the people. "What's he doing?" I thought.

Then he saw me and scurried in my direction. He came and stood in front of me about eye-level with my belt buckle. The little Brazilian orphan looked up at the big American missionary, smiled a smile that would have stolen your heart and said, "Obrigado." (Thank you.) Then, nervously scratching the back of his ankle with his big toe, he added, "*Muito* obriga-do." (Thank you *very much.*)

All of a sudden, I had a crazy craving to buy him the whole restaurant.

But before I could say anything, he turned and scampered out the door.

As I write this, I'm still standing at the coffee bar, my coffee is cold, and I'm late for my class. But I still feel the sensation that I felt half an hour ago. And I'm pondering this question: If I am so moved by a street orphan who says thank you for a piece of bread, how much more is God moved when I pause to thank him—really thank him—for saving my soul?

Tenderness

How far you go in life depends on your being tender with the young,
compassionate with the aged, sympathetic with the striving,
and tolerant of the weak and the strong—
because someday you will have been all of these.

—GEORGE WASHINGTON CARVER

SOMETHING FOR STEVIE

DAN ANDERSON

*T*ry not to be biased, but I had my doubts about hiring Stevie. His placement counselor assured me that he would be a good, reliable busboy, but…I had never had a mentally handicapped employee and wasn't sure I wanted one. I wasn't sure how my customers would react to Stevie. He was short, a little dumpy, with the smooth facial features and thick-tongued speech of Down syndrome. I wasn't worried about most of my trucker customers, because truckers don't generally care who buses tables as long as the meatloaf platter is good and the pies are homemade. The four-wheeler drivers were the ones who concerned me; the mouthy college kids traveling to school; the yuppie snobs who secretly polish their silverware with their napkins for fear of catching some dreaded "truckstop germ"; the pairs of white shirted businessmen on expense accounts who think every truckstop waitress wants to be flirted with. I knew those people would be uncomfortable around Stevie, so I closely watched him for the first few weeks.

I shouldn't have worried. After the first week, Stevie had my staff wrapped around his stubby little finger, and within a month my truck regulars had adopted him as their official truckstop mascot. After that I really didn't care what the rest of the customers thought of him. He was like a twenty-one-year-old in blue jeans and Nikes, eager to laugh and eager to please, but fierce in his attention to his duties.

Every salt and pepper shaker was exactly in its place, not a bread crumb or coffee spill was visible when Stevie got done with the table. Our only prob-

22

lem was convincing him to wait to clean a table until after the customers were finished.

He would hover in the background, shifting his weight from one foot to the other, scanning the dining room until a table was empty. Then he would scurry to the empty table and carefully bus the dishes and glasses onto the cart and meticulously wipe the table up with a practiced flourish of his rag. If he thought a customer was watching, his brow would pucker with added concentration. He took pride in doing his job exactly right, and you had to love how hard he tried to please each and every person he met.

Over time, we learned that he lived with his mother, a widow who was disabled after repeated surgeries for cancer. They lived on their Social Security benefits in public housing two miles from the truckstop.

Their social worker, who stopped to check on him every so often, admitted they had fallen between the cracks. Money was tight, and what I paid him was probably the difference between their being able to live together and Stevie's being sent to a group home.

That's why the restaurant was a gloomy place that morning last August, the first morning in three years that Stevie missed work. He was at the Mayo Clinic in Rochester getting a new valve or something put in his heart. His social worker said that people with Down syndrome often had heart problems at an early age, so this wasn't unexpected, and there was a good chance he would come through the surgery in good shape and be back at work in a few months.

A ripple of excitement ran through the staff later that morning when word came that he was out of surgery, in recovery, and doing fine. Frannie, my head waitress, let out a war whoop and did a little dance in the aisle when she heard the good news. Belle Ringer, one of our regular trucker customers, stared at the sight of the fifty-year-old grandmother of four doing a victory shimmy beside his table.

Frannie blushed, smoothed her apron, and shot Belle Ringer a withering look. He grinned. "Okay, Frannie, what was that all about?" he asked.

"We just got word that Stevie is out of surgery and going to be okay."

"I was wondering where he was. I had a new joke to tell him. What was the surgery about?"

Frannie quickly told Belle Ringer and the other two drivers sitting at his booth about Stevie's surgery, then sighed.

"Yeah, I'm glad he is going to be okay," she said, "but I don't know how he and his mom are going to handle all the bills. From what I hear, they're barely getting by as it is."

Belle Ringer nodded thoughtfully, and Frannie hurried off to wait on the rest of her tables. Since I hadn't had time to round up a busboy to replace Stevie, and really didn't want to replace him, the girls were busing their own tables that day till we decided what to do.

After the morning rush, Frannie walked into my office. She had a couple of paper napkins in her hand, a funny look on her face.

"What's up?" I asked.

"I didn't get that table where Belle Ringer and his friends were sitting cleared off after they left, and Pony Pete and Tony Tipper were sitting there when I got back to clean it off," she said. "This was folded and tucked under a coffee cup."

She handed the napkin to me, and three twenty-dollar bills fell onto my desk when I opened it. On the outside, in big, bold letters was printed "Something for Stevie."

"Pony Pete asked me what that was all about," she said, "so I told him about Stevie and his mom and everything, and Pete looked at Tony and Tony looked at Pete, and they ended up giving me this."

She handed me another paper napkin that had "Something for Stevie" scrawled on its outside. Two fifty-dollar bills were tucked within its folds. Frannie looked at me with wet, shiny eyes, shook her head and said simply "truckers."

That was three months ago. Today is Thanksgiving, the first day Stevie is supposed to be back to work. His placement worker said he's been counting the days until the doctor said he could work, and it didn't matter at all that it was a holiday. He called ten times in the past week, making sure we knew he was coming, fearful that we had forgotten him or that his job was in jeopardy.

I arranged to have his mother bring him to work, met them in the parking lot, and invited them both to celebrate his day back.

Stevie was thinner and paler but couldn't stop grinning as he pushed through the doors and headed for the back room where his apron and busing cart were waiting.

"Hold up there, Stevie, not so fast," I said. I took him and his mother by their arms. "Work can wait for a minute. To celebrate you coming back, breakfast for you and your mother is on me."

I led them toward a large corner booth at the rear of the room. I could feel and hear the rest of the staff following behind as we marched through the dining room. Glancing over my shoulder, I saw booth after booth of grinning truckers empty and join the procession.

We stopped in front of the big table. Its surface was covered with coffee cups, saucers, and dinner plates, all sitting slightly crooked on dozens of folded paper napkins.

"First thing you have to do, Stevie, is clean up this mess," I said. I tried to sound stern.

Stevie looked at me, and then at his mother, then pulled out one of the napkins. It had "Something for Stevie" printed on the outside. As he picked it up, two ten-dollar bills fell onto the table.

Stevie stared at the money, then at all the napkins peeking from beneath the tableware, each with his name printed or scrawled on it.

I turned to his mother. "There's more than ten thousand dollars in cash and checks on that table, all from truckers and trucking companies that heard about your problems. Happy Thanksgiving."

Well, it got real noisy about that time, with everybody hollering and shouting, and there were a few tears, as well. But you know what's funny?

While everybody else was busy shaking hands and hugging each other, Stevie, with a big, big smile on his face, was busy clearing all the cups and dishes from the table....

Best worker I ever hired!

You'll not likely go wrong here if you keep remembering that our Master said, "You're far happier giving than getting."

ACTS 20:35, *THE MESSAGE*

MEANINGFUL TOUCH

JOHN TRENT
FROM *LEAVING THE LIGHT ON*

he young GI stepped into line with the other teenagers to get his barbecued chicken. It's funny how some people can look eighteen—until you look at their eyes. I think it was his haunted look that caused me to notice him that evening. From the window of his eyes, he looked like a tired old man, not like the swarm of happy kids around him.

I was part of a work crew at Trail West, Young Life's beautiful camp high in the Colorado Rockies. It was my job that night to stand at the head of the line and hand out the best smelling, best tasting barbecued chicken I'd ever eaten—before or since.

We had our huge grill fired up in the middle of a large, grassy meadow, rimmed by massive, solemn pines that stood like a majestic fence around us. The sun was sliding behind the surrounding mountain peaks as the fragrant smoke from our barbecue drifted across the clearing.

It was 1969, the summer of my junior year of high school. It didn't occur to me then, but while the laughing, noisy high schoolers waited for their meal that evening, a number of their dads, friends, schoolmates, and older brothers were fighting and dying in the rice paddies and jungles of Southeast Asia.

It was easy to spot the young Nam vet in our midst. In an era of sideburns and shaggy haircuts, his government-issue "buzz-cut" drew plenty of sidelong glances. He had actually graduated from high school a couple of years before, but his parents had gotten special permission for him to attend the camp.

That's the kind of crazy war it was: Two weeks before, he'd been fighting for his life, watching buddies drop all around him. Then suddenly his tour was up, he was airlifted out of a fierce firefight to Saigon, got on a commercial airliner, and headed home. Just like that.

Now he was on leave, standing in line in a Rocky Mountain meadow with a bunch of kids who didn't seem to have a care in the world.

I first noticed him when he was about the fourth person from the front of the line. His face was extremely pale and he was visibly trembling. I remember thinking, *Something's wrong with this guy. He must be getting sick.*

As he got closer to the grill, he began shaking even harder. I picked up a piece of chicken with my tongs and was just about to serve him when he suddenly dropped his plate, spilling beans and salad on the ground and on the person in front of him. With a choked cry—he took off on a dead run for the forest.

Everyone stopped talking and just stared. We all wondered, *What in the world's wrong with him?*

Our Young Life leader headed off after the young soldier, and after they both disappeared into the trees, the dinner line resumed its onward march.

Doug found him hiding in the trees, shaking like a leaf. The older man, a burly ex-football player, towered nearly a foot above the soldier and probably outweighed him by a hundred pounds. But without saying a word, he gently put his arms around the trembling camper and held him tight.

The young soldier buried his face in our leader's chest and sobbed uncontrollably. They stood together in the twilight for nearly twenty minutes. The young man sobbing, the older man holding him, saying nothing.

When he finally was able to compose himself, they sat on a log together and the vet tried to explain what was going on.

Over in Nam, he said, if you were out in open country like that, with so many people milling around, you could expect the mortar rounds to start coming in. He had just seen his sergeant killed, right in front of him by an incoming shell. And no matter how hard he tried, he couldn't keep the sights and sounds from coming back.

Just before he reached the head of the line, it was as if he could hear the whistle of artillery fire and the screams of "Incoming! Incoming!" He couldn't take it any longer and ran to find cover.

That was day two of the camp, of what would become the most important week of this young man's life. Before the week was over, the soldier surrendered his life to a new Commander, Jesus Christ. But not for the reason you may think.

On the final night of camp, as we all sat around a big bonfire, campers were encouraged to stand up and make public their confession of faith if they had come to know Christ that week.

Many young men and women responded to the opportunity, citing talks by the speaker, the encouragement of a close friend from home, and other causes as reasons for coming to know Jesus personally. The young soldier was one of the last to stand.

His story was much different from the rest. He began by telling how skeptical he had been about coming to camp. In fact, the only reason he'd agreed to come was that his parents promised to buy him a used car. The thought of his own wheels pushed him over the edge, and he came reluctantly to camp.

While everyone had been "real nice" to him, it wasn't a special friendship that had shaped his decision. And even though he thought the speaker had some good words to say, and made the gospel clear, it wasn't because of him either that he was responding to Christ.

What had really broken through to him was "that big guy," Doug, who had been willing to stand there in the trees with him and hold him until a piece of nightmare loosened its grip. In short, God used a hug—not a lecture, not a long walk through the trees, not a testimony—to win the bigger spiritual battle he was fighting.

Sorrows

Believe me, every man has his secret sorrows
which the world knows not—
and often times we call a man cold,
when he is only sad.

—Henry Wadsworth Longfellow

THE TATTOOED STRANGER

SUSAN FAHNCKE

He was kind of scary. He sat there on the grass with his cardboard sign, his dog (actually his dog was adorable), and tattoos running up and down both arms and even on his neck. His sign proclaimed him to be "stuck and hungry" and to please help.

I'm a sucker for anyone needing help. My husband both hates and loves this quality in me.

I pulled the van over and in my rearview mirror, contemplated this man, tattoos and all. He was youngish, maybe forty. He wore one of those bandannas tied over his head, biker/pirate style. Anyone could see he was dirty and had a scraggly beard. But if you looked closer, you could see that he had neatly tucked in the black T-shirt, and his things were in a small, tidy bundle. Nobody was stopping for him. I could see the other drivers take one look and immediately focus on something else—anything else.

It was so hot out. I could see in the man's very blue eyes how dejected and tired and worn-out he felt. The sweat was trickling down his face. As I sat with the air-conditioning blowing, the Scripture suddenly popped into my head. "Inasmuch as ye have done it unto the least of these, my brethren, so ye have done it unto me."

"I reached down into my purse and extracted a ten-dollar bill. My twelve-year-old son, Nick, knew right away what I was doing. "Can I take it to him, Mom?"

"Be careful, honey." I warned and handed him the money. I watched in the mirror as he rushed over to the man, and with a shy smile, handed it to him. I saw the man, startled, stand and take the money, putting it into his back pocket. "Good," I thought to myself, "now he will at least have a hot meal tonight." I felt satisfied, proud of myself. I had made a sacrifice and now I could go on with my errands.

When Nick got back into the car, he looked at me with sad, pleading eyes. "Mom, his dog looks so hot and the man is really nice." I knew I had to do more.

"Go back and tell him to stay there, that we will be back in fifteen minutes," I told Nick. He bounded out of the car and ran to tell the tattooed stranger.

We then ran to the nearest store and bought our gifts carefully. "It can't be too heavy," I explained to the children. "He has to be able to carry it around with him." We finally settled on our purchases. A bag of "Ol' Roy" (I hoped it was good—it looked good enough for me to eat! How do they make dog food look that way?); a flavored chew-toy shaped like a bone; a water dish, bacon flavored snacks (for the dog); two bottles of water (one for the dog, one for Mr. Tattoos); and some people snacks for the man.

We rushed back to the spot where we had left him, and there he was, still waiting. And still nobody else was stopping for him. With hands shaking, I grabbed our bags and climbed out of the car, all four of my children following me, each carrying gifts. As we walked up to him, I had a fleeting moment of fear, hoping he wasn't a serial killer.

I looked into his eyes and saw something that startled me and made me ashamed of my judgment. I saw tears. He was fighting like a little boy to hold back his tears. How long had it been since someone showed this man kindness? I told him I hoped it wasn't too heavy for him to carry and showed him what we had brought. He stood there, like a child at Christmas, and I felt like my small contributions were so inadequate. When I took out the water dish, he snatched it out of my hands as if it were solid gold and told me he had had no way to give his dog water. He gingerly set it down, filled it with the bottled water we brought, and stood up to look directly into my eyes. His were so blue, so intense, and my own filled with tears as he said, "Ma'am, I don't know what to say." He then put both hands on his bandanna-clad head and just started to cry. This man, this "scary" man, was so gentle, so sweet, so humble.

I smiled through my tears and said, "Don't say anything." Then I noticed the tattoo on his neck. It said "Mama tried."

As we all piled into the van and drove away, he was on his knees, arms around his dog, kissing his nose and smiling. I waved cheerfully and then finally broke down in tears.

I have so much. My worries seem so trivial and petty now. I have a home, a loving husband, four beautiful children. I have a bed. I wondered where he would sleep tonight.

My stepdaughter, Brandie, turned to me and said in the sweetest little-girl voice, "I feel so good."

Although it seemed as if we had helped him, the man with the tattoos gave us a gift that I will never forget. He taught that no matter what the outside looks like, inside each of us is a human being deserving of kindness, of compassion, of acceptance. He opened my heart.

Tonight and every night I will pray for the gentle man with the tattoos and his dog. And I will hope that God will send more people like him into my life to remind me what's really important.

If anyone has material possessions
and sees his brother in need but has no pity on him,
how can the love of God be in him?

1 JOHN 3:17

Last Week

Last week
my friend wept
and prayed in agony.
I knew it
and I love my friend.
Still, I offered
neither tears nor help.
I could only wait
suspended
until God heard
her prayers.
They were for me.

DOROTHY PURDY
FROM *FANFARE*

THE PAXTON HOTEL

CHRIS FABRY

FROM *AT THE CORNER OF MUNDANE AND GRACE*

A few years ago a fire destroyed the Paxton Hotel in downtown Chicago. Those of us in the suburbs watched the news and felt bad for the victims and their families, but a couple of days later we tired of the investigation. I worked a few blocks from the hotel and watched the fire engines and the snarled traffic from my office window. The grim search for bodies was unsettling.

A day or two later, I began to think about her. I didn't know her name. She didn't show up every day or even every week, but she was a fixture in our lobby.

She wore long pullover sweaters and polyester pants that swished when she walked. Her matted hair, once dark, was turning gray. Her shoes were held together by threads and a prayer. It seemed her only friend was the coat she wore in every season, even in the dead of summer.

Her most distinguishing feature was her voice. When she talked, you could hear the sound reverberate off the high ceiling and through the elevator shaft. Often she talked to herself. She laughed.

At times she scared me. Her eyes were piercing brown. Once I was on the elevator with about fifteen elderly visitors. She stepped on at the lower level, and we were shoved close together. I held my breath.

She panned the crowd of stooped and withering men and women and quoted her King James version of the Bible.

"Looks like we've got a bunch of hoary heads," she crackled. "That means white head."

I smiled to those around us, hoping they would understand this was not an employee but an intruder. She laughed again loudly and shook her head. The people didn't seem to mind.

I remember walking in one day and seeing her sitting at the entrance by the elevators. I passed her quickly, pushed the "up" button, and darted toward the water fountain around the corner. I stayed there until the familiar ding of the elevator bell signaled my deliverance. I stepped through the door and turned around to see her talking and laughing. The room was empty except for the receptionist. The woman talked to the wall. When the door closed, I rolled my eyes and sighed. I had dodged her again.

I was thinking about these moments when a co-worker stepped into my office. I mentioned this lady and asked if he knew her. "Sure," he said. "She comes to our church. She's always asking the receptionist about her make-up. Says she can't do a thing with her hair." And then he said the words that made my heart sink. "I heard she was living at the Paxton."

His phone rang and he left me staring out the window. She was living at the Paxton?

"I didn't even know her name," I said out loud.

We are all a little crazy, I thought. There probably isn't much difference between what goes on in my head and what came from her mouth. She was just different.

God left me here in the midst of messy people's lives for a purpose. Too often I'm just concerned about myself. If I could ride the elevator with her again or see her in the corner staring out the window, I believe I would treat her more kindly. Maybe I'll have the chance today to meet someone like her. Maybe then I'll get it right and ask her name.

The Lord does not look at the things man looks at.
Man looks at the outward appearance,
but the Lord looks at the heart.

1 SAMUEL 16:7

ROOKIE DRIVER

CHARLES R. SWINDOLL
FROM *IMPROVING YOUR SERVE*

'll call this young man Aaron, not his real name. Late one spring he was praying about having a significant ministry the following summer. He asked God for a position to open up on some church staff or Christian organization. Nothing happened. Summer arrived, still nothing. Days turned into weeks, and Aaron finally faced reality—he needed any job he could find. He checked the want ads and the only thing that seemed to be a possibility was driving a bus in southside Chicago—nothing to brag about, but it would help with tuition in the fall. After learning the route, he was on his own—a rookie driver in a dangerous section of the city. It wasn't long before Aaron realized just how dangerous his job really was.

A small gang of tough kids spotted the young driver, and began to take advantage of him. For several mornings in a row they got on, walked right past him without paying, ignored his warnings, and rode until they decided to get off...all the while making smart remarks to him and others on the bus. Finally, he decided it had gone on long enough.

The next morning, after the gang got on as usual, Aaron saw a policeman on the next corner, so he pulled over and reported the offense. The officer told them to pay or get off. They paid but, unfortunately, the policeman got off. And they stayed on. When the bus turned another corner or two, the gang assaulted the young driver.

When he came to, blood was all over his shirt, two teeth were missing, both eyes were swollen, his money was gone, and the bus was empty. After returning to the terminal and being given the weekend off, our friend went to his little apartment, sank onto his bed, and stared at the ceiling in disbelief. Resentful thoughts swarmed his mind. Confusion, anger, and disillusionment added fuel to the fire of his physical pain. He spent a fitful night wrestling with the Lord.

How can this be? Where's God in all of this? I genuinely want to serve Him. I prayed for a ministry. I was willing to serve Him anywhere, doing anything, and this is the thanks I get!

On Monday morning Aaron decided to press charges. With the help of the officer who had encountered the gang and several who were willing to testify as witnesses against the thugs, most of them were rounded up and taken to the local county jail. Within a few days there was a hearing before the judge.

In walked Aaron and his attorney plus the angry gang members who glared across the room in his direction. Suddenly he was seized with a whole new series of thoughts. Not bitter ones, but compassionate ones! His heart went out to the guys who had attacked him. Under the Spirit's control he no longer hated them—he pitied them. They needed help, not more hate. What could he do or say?

Suddenly, after there was a plea of guilty, Aaron (to the surprise of his attorney and everybody else in the courtroom) stood to his feet and requested permission to speak.

"Your Honor, I would like you to total up all the days of punishment against these men—all the time sentenced against them—and I request that you allow me to go to jail in their place."

The judge didn't know whether to spit or wind his watch. Both attorneys were stunned. As Aaron looked over at the gang members (whose mouths and eyes looked like saucers), he smiled and said quietly, "It's because I forgive you."

The dumbfounded judge, when he reached a level of composure, said rather firmly: "Young man, you're out of order. This sort of thing has never been done before!" To which the young man replied with genius insight:

"Oh, yes, it has, your honor…yes, it has. It happened over nineteen centuries ago when a man from Galilee paid the penalty that all mankind deserved."

And then, for the next three or four minutes, without interruption, he explained how Jesus Christ died on our behalf, thereby proving God's love and forgiveness.

He was not granted his request, but the young man visited the gang members in jail, led most of them to faith in Christ, and began a significant ministry to many others in southside Chicago.

CHARLIE'S BLANKET

WENDY MILLER
FROM *CHRISTMAS IN MY HEART*

ary hurried to get her children fed and dressed. It was a cold December day, and they had a long way to walk. Mary cleaned houses five days a week; it was the only work she could find that would allow her to also take care of her three small girls at the same time. She would drop the older two off at the elementary school and take 3-year-old Becky with her. The girls came to her for lunch, and she would be back home again before they were home from school in the afternoon. It was a good arrangement, and it kept her off welfare. She wanted help from no one.

"Becky," she called, "hurry; we're all ready to go!"

Becky ran to the door, a ragged doll with all its hair loved off cradled in her arms. "I'm all ready, Mama, but we forgot to dress Charlie."

Mary glanced at the clock and back down at her daughter's smiling face. Quickly she dressed the doll, wrapped it in its blanket, and handed it back to Becky. Then the little family went out into the cold, dark early morning.

"Mama,"—Laura, 7, and the oldest, took Mary's hand—"I'm sorry I forgot Charlie. Are we awfully late?"

"No, Laura, we're not awfully late."

"I don't know why we have to dress that stupid doll of hers anyway," complained Cindy. Since she was 6 and in the first grade, she thought of herself as all grown up—and to her, Charlie was a big waste of time.

Two years ago Mary might have agreed with her. They had been well-off then and wanted for nothing. Mary's thoughts traveled back to other times and compared then to now as she had done a million times. One day everything was fine, and the next day her husband was gone. All he had left behind was a note to say goodbye. No, he had also left behind a wife, three small girls, and an empty bank account.

As soon as the shock had worn off, Mary tried to start a new life, but it was so hard. She had never had to work outside the home before. Now she was cleaning houses to keep the girls fed. Their clothes were handed down from her employers' children. Most of all she regretted having to make them walk so far every day, especially in the cold.

As for the radical change in lifestyle, the girls had just accepted it as part of life. Laura and Cindy helped as much as they could and tried not to complain. Becky found happiness in her doll. Charlie was her whole world. She never quit smiling as long as she had Charlie. He was always to be dressed for the weather and then wrapped in the precious blanket. It was just an old scrap of a blanket that someone must have dropped in the parking lot; Becky had found it there, Mary washed it, and now it was Charlie's. Was Charlie a waste of time? No, Mary decided; he was Becky's happiness, and that most certainly was not a waste of time.

As they neared the school, the girls hugged Mary as they always did day after day, then ran in. Farther down the street, Mary turned in at the Littles'—Monday's house. The Littles had been getting ready for Christmas, it seemed, because there was a wreath on the door with a big red bow. Mary was prepared to see all the fancy trimmings inside. Becky wasn't.

"Ooh, Charlie," she whispered as if afraid that her voice might disturb the splendor, "Look at what Mrs. Little got." The room was gaily decorated for Christmas, and in the corner stood a huge Christmas tree. The silver star shining on the top almost touched the ceiling. Glass ornaments, garlands, and tinsel were tastefully arranged on the branches, and underneath was a mountain of parcels wrapped in ribbons and bows.

Mary took Becky's coat and hung it up. The little girl just stood looking at the tree. "Becky, I have to get to work now. Promise you won't touch anything."

"I promise, Mama." And she crawled into a big easy chair, and there she stayed for the entire morning, pointing out the pretty ornaments to Charlie and guessing what might be in each of the packages.

Laura and Cindy came in at lunch, but they hardly looked at the tree. It hurt to look at it. They knew that there would be no tree for them—just like last year. Money was not to be spent on anything they could do without. They knew it—but it still hurt.

The day replayed itself on Tuesday at the Johnsons', on Wednesday at the Harrises', Thursday at the Krebbs', and Friday at the Fishers'. But on Saturday they were home.

After spending a week in the various houses all decked in glorious holiday fashion, Becky suddenly seemed to realize that she was missing out on something. "Why does everyone have a tree in the house, Mama? Why are there so many presents? Is it somebody's birthday? Why don't we have a tree?"

Mary had known the question would be asked. Laura and Cindy looked up from the floor where they were playing, waiting for her answer. Mary put away her mending and pulled Becky up onto her lap. "You're a very smart girl. It is somebody's birthday, and I'll tell you all about Him. His name is Jesus, and He was born Christmas Day." And Mary told the girls how it came to happen and why there is Christmas.

Becky hugged Charlie close. "Ooh, the poor Baby. Was it very cold in the stable? I wouldn't want to sleep in a stable, would you? I wish I could go there and see it, though."

"We can see it," Mary said, and she put her daughter off her knee. "Girls, get your coats on. We're going for a walk."

Down the street was a church. Every Christmas a large creche was set up. There was a wooden stable full of straw and large ceramic figures. High above hung a star. The girls were awed by the simple but beautiful scene. It was just as Mary had said it was from the story in the Bible. Becky didn't want to leave even when the cold seeped through her clothing and made her shiver.

The next week was just as hard for them. Everywhere they went, it seemed that the world was taunting them with a Christmas that wasn't theirs. In the malls carols played, and parents loaded up with the latest toys and games. As Mary picked out economy packs of socks and underwear for the girls' gifts, she tried not to look in the other carts. At Safeway she whipped through the express line with one lone pack of spaghetti for their Christmas dinner. She laughed at the long line-ups of people with their carts full of turkey and fixings. But the laugh was hollow, because she would have loved to be one of those standing in line. Outside, families shouted and laughed as they picked out what each considered the perfect tree and then strapped it to the roof of their car. Mary tried not to notice. It was Laura and Cindy that finally made her heart well over with bitterness.

Somehow, when you are an adult, you can take whatever is dished out. You take things in stride and make the best of a situation. But, oh how different it is when your child is hurting! Nothing hurts a mother more than the sorrow of her child. And that's how it was with Mary. The school was focused on Christmas, which was only to be expected in December. The teachers had the children making ornaments and stringing up popcorn for their trees at home. They wrote letters to Santa. At recess, the children told of the gifts they were expecting. Laura and Cindy said nothing. They did as they were expected in class and tried to avoid the other children at recess. It was at home that they expressed their hurt and anger at the world for leaving them out of Christmas. So the bitterness grew in Mary from the heartache of her girls.

Every carol and decoration seemed to make her colder. Every Christmas card or call of "Merry Christmas" made her hate the season more. Laura and Cindy, taking the cue from their mother as children often do, developed the same attitude. Only little Becky remained immune. She rocked Charlie in her arms and told him again and again about Baby Jesus, who was born in a stable. She begged the girls daily to take her to the church so she could see the story "for true." They would take her grudgingly and drag her back home long before she was finished looking.

Christmas morning came in a flurry of snow. Laura and Cindy woke up cold. They ran into Mary's room and burrowed under the covers with her to warm up. Mary cuddled them close and kissed their foreheads.

"Merry Christmas," she said.

"Merry Christmas, Mama," they echoed.

"I'm afraid there aren't a lot of gifts for you girls, but you go wake up Becky, and you can open what there is," she said resignedly.

The girls jumped out of the bed and ran to get their sister while Mary got up and dressed. Too soon, they were back.

"Where is she, Mama? We can't find her!" The words hit Mary like a truck. The three raced through the house calling her name, checking every closet and corner. They checked the yard and the neighbor's yard. No Becky! They must have missed her when they checked the house, Mary thought. She never goes off alone. They searched the house again.

"Dear Lord, please help me find her," she prayed as she rechecked every spot a child could possibly be in. "I'm sorry for my selfishness. The gifts and the dinner that I prayed for are not important. Forget them and just give me back my Becky." She was frantic now.

Then she noticed Charlie. He was carefully positioned in a chair facing a window. Mary's heart raced with her thoughts. Charlie was never out of Becky's sight. And where was his blanket? Becky always insisted that his blanket be wrapped tightly around him at all times. Suddenly she knew!

"Stay here!" she admonished the girls as she flew out the door into the dark and snowy morning. Down the street she ran, until she could see the church. Then she slowed, and tears of release ran down her face as she caught sight of her daughter. The star from the creche was shining down on the manger where Becky had climbed in and was busily covering the Baby Jesus with the ratty scrap of a blanket. As she neared, Mary could hear Becky talking:

"You must be cold. I knew the snow would be falling on you. This is Charlie's blanket, but we will give it to you. He has me to keep him warm." She looked up when she heard footsteps. "Oh! Hi, Mama." Becky smiled her beautiful innocent smile. "I was afraid He might have thought we forgot Him on His birthday."

Mary plucked her out of the straw and held her tight, the tears now raining unchecked. "I did forget, Honey... Dear, I'm sorry I forgot." Then she tenderly carried her daughter home, filled at last with Christmas joy.

With Christmas carols to cheer them on, they hung the popcorn strings and ornaments on Mary's tallest houseplant. A star made of tin foil perched on the top. They put the presents underneath, and there was just enough to fit nicely under the little tree. And best of all, Mary made a birthday cake. With their hands joined around the table, they all sang "Happy Birthday, Dear Jesus, happy birthday to you...."

As for Charlie, cradled tightly in Becky's arms—even without his blanket, he was warm.

THE OLD FISHERMAN

AUTHOR UNKNOWN

Our house was directly across the street from the clinic entrance of Johns Hopkins Hospital in Baltimore. We lived downstairs and rented the upstairs rooms to outpatients at the clinic.

One summer evening as I was fixing supper, there was a knock at the door. I opened it to see a truly awful looking man. "Why, he's hardly taller than my eight-year-old," I thought as I stared at the stooped, shriveled body.

But the appalling thing was his face—lopsided from swelling, red and raw.

Yet his voice was pleasant as he said, "Good evening. I've come to see if you've a room for just one night. I came for a treatment this morning from the eastern shore, and there's no bus till morning." He told me he'd been hunting for a room since noon but with no success—no one seemed to have a room. "I guess it's my face…I know it looks terrible, but my doctor says with a few more treatments…"

For a moment I hesitated, but his next words convinced me: "I could sleep in this rocking chair on the porch. My bus leaves early in the morning."

I told him we would find him a bed, but to rest on the porch. Meanwhile, I went inside and finished getting supper. When we were ready,

I asked the old man if he would join us. "No, thank you. I have plenty." And he held up a brown paper bag.

When I had finished the dishes, I went out on the porch to talk with him a few minutes. It didn't take long to see that this man had an oversized heart crowded into that tiny body. He told me he fished for a living to support his daughter, her five children, and her husband, who was hopelessly crippled from a back injury. He didn't tell it by way of complaint; in fact, every other sentence was prefaced with a thanks to God for a blessing. He was grateful that no pain accompanied his disease, which was apparently a form of skin cancer. He thanked God for giving him the strength to keep going.

At bedtime, we put a camp cot in the children's room for him. When I got up in the morning, the bed linens were neatly folded and the little man was out on the porch. He refused breakfast, but just before he left for his bus, haltingly, as if asking a great favor, he said, "Could I please come back and stay the next time I have a treatment? I won't put you out a bit. I can sleep fine in a chair." He paused for a moment and then added, "Your children made me feel at home. Grownups are bothered by my face, but children don't seem to mind."

I told him he was welcome to come again. And on his next trip he arrived a little after seven in the morning. As a gift, he brought a big fish and a quart of the largest oysters I had ever seen. He said he had shucked them that morning before he had left so that they'd be nice and fresh. I knew his bus left at 4:00 A.M., and I wondered what time he had to get up in order to do this for us.

In the years he came to stay overnight with us there was never a time that he did not bring us fish or oysters or vegetables from his garden. Other times we received packages in the mail, always special delivery; fish and oysters packed in a box of fresh young spinach or kale, every leaf carefully washed. Knowing that he must walk three miles to mail these, and how little money he had, made the gifts doubly precious. When I received these little remembrances, I often thought of a comment our next-door neighbor made after he left that first morning. "Did you keep that awful looking man last night? I turned him away! You can lose roomers by putting up such people!"

Maybe we did lose roomers once or twice. But oh!—if only they could have known him, perhaps their illnesses would have been easier to bear. I know our family always will be grateful to have known him; from him we learned what it was to accept the bad without complaint and the good with gratitude to God.

Recently, I was visiting a friend who has a greenhouse. As she showed me her flowers, we came to the most beautiful one of all—a golden chrysanthemum, bursting with blooms. But to my great surprise, it was growing in an old dented, rusty bucket. I thought to myself, "If this were my plant, I'd put it in the loveliest container I had!"

My friend changed my mind. "I ran short of pots," she explained, "and knowing how beautiful this one would be, I thought it wouldn't mind starting out in this old pail. It's just for a little while, till I can put it out in the garden."

She must have wondered why I laughed so delightedly, but I was imagining just such a scene in heaven. "Here's an especially beautiful one," God might have said when he came to the soul of the sweet old fisherman. "He won't mind starting in this small body."

All this happened long ago—and now, in God's garden, how tall this lovely soul must stand.

COSTLY LOVE

*Costly love can bring new meaning to the simplest act,
both for the one giving and the one receiving.*

—DAVID AND HEATHER KOPP
FROM *LOVE STORIES GOD TOLD*

THE CHRISTMAS ROSE

Lt. Colonel Marlene Chase
From *The War Cry*
National publication of The Salvation Army

A light snow was falling as she turned the key to open Rose's Flower Shop. The name didn't take much imagination, but then it was better than "Rosie's Posies" as Clint had suggested when she had first begun business.

"Going to the Towers again this year?" asked Cass Gunther, who was opening the European deli next door.

Rose nodded. It was what they did every year. Supper and drinks at the club and Christmas Eve at the posh Park Towers. Swimming. The hot tub. Maybe take in a show. It was a tradition.

She turned on the lights, feeling bone tired. As usual, people waited until the last minute to place their Christmas orders. Why did she do this every year? It wasn't the money, though business had gone well. It filled her days, and there was something soothing about working with flowers.

"I'll be home for Christmas…" the sentimental lyric wafted from the radio under the counter. Home was four extravagantly decorated walls which she welcomed at the end of the day, but when it came down to it, what was there for her really? Perhaps if they'd been able to have children. They'd had a reasonably good marriage, the best house on Carriage Drive, money in the bank, and enough friends to keep them from feeling lonely. And goodness knows they were too busy to think about whether or not they were happy. Bills for the mortgage, the car and boat and a half dozen credit cards never stopped.

Rose sighed. A hollowness plagued her. Even anticipating Clint's surprise when he would receive the Pendleton sport coat she'd bought held little joy. His gift to her would be something beautiful, expensive…but she couldn't remember last year's gift or when they had taken time to really talk to each other.

She felt suddenly at odds, cross. Perhaps if they'd kept up with the family. But family meant Clint's two aunts in Virginia and her stepfather in Wyoming, none of whom seemed famished for their company. Hungry, that was it. She'd forgotten to eat breakfast.

The bell over the door announced a customer, but she kept her back to the counter, consulting the order book.

"Excuse me, Miss," an elderly voice called from behind her.

I haven't been a Miss in fourteen years, thank you. She swallowed the caustic retort and turned slowly to find an old man smiling at her.

He had all his teeth, a look of kind apology and a full head of wavy white hair. He held a plaid cap across his chest and gave her a quaint little bow like an aging Sir Galahad. "I'm looking for some flowers—for my wife."

At those words, something luminous lit him from within. She wondered if Clint ever looked that way when he spoke about her. "I see," she said slowly, waiting.

He tapped gnarled fingers over his cap in meditation and with warm authority in his raspy voice said, "Not just any flowers. It must be Christmas roses."

"Well, we have roses. American beauty reds, pink, tea and yellow—"

"Oh, no," he said, shifting his negligible weight from one foot to the other. "Christmas roses—white as snow—with some of that feathery fern tucked in. And I'd like a big red bow, too."

"It's Christmas Eve, sir, and I'm afraid we're fresh out—"

"My wife loves white roses," he continued, looking at something she couldn't see. "They remind her of the Babe of Christmas and the purity of His heart. She hasn't seen any roses for such a long time. And now that—"

The old man's shoulders drooped ever so slightly, then straightened again. Rose heard the faint tremor and was touched by something beautiful in the old face that made her think of alabaster. No, alabaster was too cold.

"She's ill now…" He paused and tucked his cap under his arm. "We served at a medical clinic in West Africa for more than thirty years. But we've had to return home. Nell has Alzheimer's. We're living at Country Gardens—"

"Oh, I'm sorry," Rose breathed.

The man rushed on without a trace of bitterness. "I have a little room on the floor just below the nursing wing where Nell is. We share meals together—and we have our memories. God has been good to us."

Rose returned his smile, uncomprehending, but unable to deny the man's sincerity. White roses on Christmas Eve? She might be able to get them from Warrensville, but it would be a stretch.

"We'll be spending Christmas Eve in my room—just the two of us— a celebration," he was saying. "Christmas roses for Nell would make it perfect."

"I may be able to get them sent over from Warrensville—" Rose bit her lip. *Was she crazy? It would take a miracle. Then there was the price.* "How much do you want to spend?"

The man set his cap on the counter and dug out a faded wallet from trousers that had seen several winters. He pushed four five-dollar bills toward her with childlike eagerness, then seeing her dismay, hesitated. "I hope it's enough."

"I could give you a nice spray of red roses in a bud vase," Rose began. *White rose centerpieces would start at thirty-five dollars. Then the delivery charge would run another twenty, especially on Christmas Eve. If she could get them!*

"I had hoped for a real special bouquet—" he broke off, and she read his profound disappointment.

"Leave it to me. I'll do my best to get you something nice," she began, astounded by her own words.

"Bless you!" the old man said, reaching across the counter and grasping her hands. "Can they be delivered around four or five? It will be such a surprise! I can't thank you enough." Nearly dancing, he replaced his cap and began backing toward the door. "Arnold Herriman—Room 7! Merry Christmas! God bless you! God bless you!"

What had a tired old man with a sick wife have to be so happy about? She puzzled over that through the next few orders, then placed a call to a supplier in Warrensville. They could get her a dozen white roses at $42.50—but it would be four o'clock before they could be relayed to her shop.

"Okay," she said wearily, realizing that she herself would have to deliver the Christmas roses to Mr. Herriman. No matter. Clint would likely be delayed by a promising client.

The flowers arrived at ten minutes to four and Rose quickly arranged them in a silver bowl, tucking in the feathery greens and sprigs of baby's breath and holly. She secured a lacy red bow into the base and balanced it in one hand while locking the door with the other.

Country Gardens hardly resembled its name. Surely a couple who'd spent a lifetime healing the sick in an obscure village deserved better in the sunset of their years.

She found the residential wing and tentatively approached number 7. Arnold Herriman in the same old trousers and shirt with a crimson tie beamed at her. She entered a room with a few pieces of old furniture and walls bursting with pictures and certificates. On the hall table was a creche. *The Babe of Christmas and the purity of His heart,* Herriman had said.

A diminutive woman sat on the sofa with hands folded over a patchwork quilt on her lap. She had a translucent complexion and vacant blue eyes above two brightly rouged cheeks. A bit of red ribbon had been tucked into her white hair. Her eyes widened when she saw the flowers, then spilled over with tears.

"Nell, darling. It's your surprise—Christmas roses," Arnold said, placing an arm around the woman's fragile shoulders.

"Oh, how lovely!" Nell stretched out her arms, her face transformed in radiance. She rubbed one wrinkled cheek against the delicate petals, then turned a watery gaze on Rose. "Do I know you, dear?"

"This is the nice lady from the flower shop who made your bouquet," Arnold said.

"Can you stay for a while, dear?" she asked. "We'll be finished with our patients soon, and we'll take you to our house for tea."

"Oh, no—" said Rose.

Arnold touched his wife's shoulder. "The patients are all gone, dear. We're home, and it's Christmas Eve."

Rose's throat ached with unshed tears and the sense that something beautiful lived here from which she was excluded. Could it be that in living their lives for others these two old people who had nothing but each other and a bouquet of white roses had everything that was important?

Suddenly Nell plucked one of the long-stemmed white roses from the elegant bouquet and held it out to Rose. "Please, I have so many. You must take one for yourself!"

"Yes," Arnold said, taking the stem from his wife and pressing it toward her, "Thank you for all your trouble. God bless you."

She wanted to say that He already had, that bringing them the Christmas roses had made her happier than she could remember in a long time, that on this Christmas Eve she had learned something of the meaning of the holiday she had missed until now.

Many waters cannot quench love; rivers cannot wash it away.
Song of Songs 8:7

More Beautiful

The question is asked, "Is there anything more beautiful in life than a boy and girl clasping clean hands and pure hearts in the path of marriage? Can there be anything more beautiful than young love?"

And the answer is given. "Yes, there is a more beautiful thing. It is the spectacle of an old man and an old woman finishing their journey together on that path. Their hands are gnarled, but still clasped; their faces are seamed, but still radiant; their hearts are physically bowed and tired, but still strong with love and devotion for one another. Yes, there is a more beautiful thing than young love. Old love."

AUTHOR UNKNOWN

LOVE LETTER
FROM HEAVEN

LUCILLE HEIMRICH
FROM *A MATCH MADE IN HEAVEN*

*S*everal years ago my husband, George, died of complications following an automobile accident. Ours had been a long, happy marriage, and his death left me deeply depressed. As time passed, instead of being grateful for all the wonderful years we'd shared, I became engulfed in self-pity. Often I prayed, "Lord, why didn't you take me first?"

When I broke my leg a few weeks before my ninetieth birthday, I felt more confined—and alone—than ever. "If only George was here," I despaired, "he would chase away this sadness with words of wisdom and encouragement."

On this particularly blue day, I decided to call a friend and ask her to visit. Unfortunately, she was leaving on a trip and couldn't come.

I understood. But as I hung up the phone, tears started to flow. I moved to the window to sit in my favorite chair with Duke, my beloved cat, curled up in my lap. "Dear God," I prayed, weeping, "please give me the strength to get through this hour."

Get your Bible, a quiet voice inside me nudged. But my Bible was in the bedroom, and with my leg in a cast, it would be too hard to retrieve. Then I remembered my small travel Bible. Hadn't I seen it on the living room bookshelf? I found it and opened it, surprised to discover that it was George's old travel Bible instead of mine. They looked alike, and I thought I'd given his Bible away.

I turned the pages until I reached my favorite Scripture. Suddenly a letter fell into my lap. Carefully I unfolded the yellowed pages. It was a love letter from George. In it, he expressed his deep affection for me. His words of comfort went straight to my lonely heart.

My cheeks wet with tears, I continued to leaf through the Bible. In the back pages I found more notes from George. According to the date, he'd written these in the hospital prior to an early surgery. He must have feared that he would not return home. After he recovered from the surgery, the letter and notes were forgotten.

But no, I realized. They were *never* forgotten. God knew exactly where George's words of comfort were hidden—and exactly when I'd need them the most. Laughing some and crying some, I spent the rest of the afternoon basking in the company of both my husband's letters and my Lord. I never felt less alone, and now I knew for certain that I never would be.

Train Our Love

Train our love
that it may grow
slowly…deeply…steadily;
till our hearts will overflow
unrestrained and readily.
Discipline it, too,
dear God;
strength of steel
throughout the whole.
Teach us patience,
thoughtfulness,
tenderness, and
self-control.
Deepen it
throughout the years,
age and mellow it
until, time that finds us
old without,
within,
will find us
lovers still.

—RUTH BELL GRAHAM
FROM *COLLECTED POEMS*

CHRISTMAS LOST
AND FOUND

SHIRLEY BARKSDALE
FROM *McCALL'S* MAGAZINE

We called him our Christmas Boy, because he came to us during that season of joy, when he was just six days old. Already his eyes twinkled more brightly than the lights on his first tree.

Later, as our family expanded, he made it clear that only he had the expertise to select and decorate the tree each year. He rushed the season, starting his gift list before we'd even finished the Thanksgiving turkey. He pressed us into singing carols, our croaky voices sounding more froglike than ever compared to his perfect pitch. He stirred us up, led us through a round of merry chaos.

Then, on his twenty-fourth Christmas, he left us as unexpectedly as he had come. A car accident on an icy Denver street, on his way home to his young wife and infant daughter. But first he had stopped by the family home to decorate our tree, a ritual he had never abandoned.

Without his invincible Yuletide spirit, we were like poorly trained dancers, unable to perform after the music had stopped. In our grief, his father and I sold our home, where memories clung to every room. We moved to California, leaving behind our support system of friends and church. All the wrong moves.

It seemed I had come full circle, back to those early years when there had been just my parents and me. Christmas had always been a quiet, hurried affair, unlike the celebrations at my friends' homes, which were lively and peopled with rollicking relatives. I vowed then that someday I'd marry and have six children, and that at Christmas my house would vibrate with energy and love.

I found the man who shared my dream, but we had not reckoned on the surprise of infertility. Undaunted, we applied for adoption, ignoring gloomy prophecies that an adopted child would not be the same as "our own flesh and blood." Even then, hope did not run high; the waiting list was long. But against all odds, within a year he arrived and was ours. Then nature surprised us again, and in rapid succession we added two biological children to the family. Not as many as we had hoped for, but compared to my quiet childhood, three made an entirely satisfactory crowd.

Those friends were right about adopted children not being the same. He wasn't the least like the rest of us. Through his own unique heredity, he brought color into our lives with his gift of music, his irrepressible good cheer, his bossy wit. He made us look and behave better than we were.

In the sixteen years that followed his death, time added chapters to our lives. His widow remarried and had a son; his daughter graduated from high school. His brother married and began his own Christmas traditions in another state. His sister, an artist, seemed fulfilled by her career. His father and I grew old enough to retire, and in Christmas of 1987 we decided to return to Denver. The call home was unclear; we knew only that we yearned for some indefinable connection, for something lost that had to be retrieved before time ran out.

We slid into Denver on the tail end of a blizzard. Blocked highways forced us through the city, past the Civic Center, ablaze with thousands of lights—a scene I was not ready to face. This same trek had been one of our Christmas Boy's favorite holiday traditions. He had been relentless in his insistence that we all pile into the car, its windows fogged over with our warm breath, its tires fighting for a grip in ice.

I looked away from the lights and fixed my gaze on the distant Rockies, where he had loved to go barreling up the mountainside in search of the perfect tree. Now in the foothills there was his grave—a grave I could not bear to visit.

Once we were settled in the small, boxy house, so different from the family home where we had orchestrated our lives, we hunkered down like two barn swallows who had missed the last migration south. While I stood staring toward the snowcapped mountains one day, I heard the sudden screech of car brakes, then the impatient peal of the doorbell. There stood our granddaughter, and in the gray-green eyes and impudent grin I saw the reflection of our Christmas Boy.

Behind her, lugging a large pine tree, came her mother, stepfather, and nine-year-old half-brother. They swept past us in a flurry of laughter; they uncorked the sparkling cider and toasted our homecoming. Then they decorated the tree and piled gaily wrapped packages under the boughs.

"You'll recognize the ornaments," said my former daughter-in-law. "They were his. I saved them for you."

"I picked out most of the gifts, Grandma," said the nine-year-old, whom I hardly knew.

When I murmured, in remembered pain, that we hadn't had a tree for, well, sixteen years, our cheeky granddaughter said, "Then it's time to shape up!"

They left in a whirl, shoving one another out the door, but not before asking us to join them the next morning for church, then dinner at their home.

"Oh, we just can't," I began.

"You sure can," ordered our granddaughter, as bossy as her father had been. "I'm singing the solo, and I want to see you there."

"Bring earplugs," advised the nine-year-old.

We had long ago given up the poignant Christmas services, but now, under pressure, we sat rigid in the front pew, fighting back tears.

Then it was solo time. Our granddaughter swished (her father would have swaggered) to center stage, and the magnificent voice soared, clear and true, in perfect pitch. She sang "O Holy Night," which brought back bittersweet memories. In a rare emotional response, the congregation applauded in delight. How her father would have relished the moment!

We had been alerted that there would be a "whole mess of people" for dinner—but thirty-five? Assorted relatives filled every corner of the house; small children, noisy and exuberant, seemed to bounce off the walls. I could not sort out who belonged to whom, but it didn't matter. They all belonged to one another. They took us in, enfolded us in joyous camaraderie. We sang carols in loud, off-key voices, saved only by that amazing soprano.

Sometime after dinner, before the winter sunset, it occurred to me that a true family is not always one's own flesh and blood. It is a climate of the heart. Had it not been for our adopted son, we would not now be surrounded by caring strangers who would help us to hear the music again.

Later, not yet ready to give up the day, our granddaughter asked us to come along with her. "I'll drive," she said.

"There's a place I like to go." She jumped behind the wheel of the car and, with the confidence of a newly licensed driver, zoomed off toward the foothills.

Alongside the headstone rested a small, heart-shaped rock, slightly cracked, painted by our artist daughter. On its weathered surface she had written: "To my brother, with love." Across the crest of the grave lay a holly-bright Christmas wreath. Our number-two son admitted, when asked, that he sent one every year.

In the chilly but somehow comforting silence, we were not prepared for our unpredictable granddaughter's next move. Once more that day her voice, so like her father's lifted in song, and the mountainside echoed the chorus of "Joy to the World," on and on into infinity.

When the last pure note had faded, I felt, for the first time since our son's death, a sense of peace, of the positive continuity of life, of renewed faith and hope. The real meaning of Christmas had been restored to us. Hallelujah!

I waited patiently for God to help me; then he listened and heard my cry. He lifted me out of the pit of despair, out from the bog and the mire, and set my feet on a hard, firm path, and steadied me as I walked along. He has given me a new song to sing, of praises to our God.

PSALM 40:1–3, *THE LIVING BIBLE*

NIGHTTIME TREASURES

FROM *GOD'S LITTLE DEVOTIONAL BOOK*

*T*wo brothers farmed together. They lived in separate houses on the family farm, but met each day in the fields to work together. One brother married and had a large family. The other lived alone. Still, they divided the harvest from the fields equally.

One night the single brother thought, *My brother is struggling to support a large family, but I get half of the harvest.* With love in his heart, he gathered a box of things he had purchased from his earnings—items he knew would help his brother's family. He planned to slip over to his brother's shed, unload the basket there, and never say a word about it.

The same night, the married brother thought, *My brother is alone. He doesn't know the joys of a family.* Out of love, he decided to take over a basket with a quilt and homemade bread and preserves to "warm" his brother's house. He planned to leave the items on his porch and never say a word.

As the brothers stealthily made their way to each other's home, they bumped into one another. They were forced to admit to what they were doing and there in the darkness, they cried and embraced, each man realizing that his greatest wealth was a brother who respected and loved him.

SOMEONE WITH YOU

LARRY LIBBY

FROM *SOMEONE WITH YOU*

Did you ever have a very, very favorite book? If you did, then you probably knew those pages so well that when someone was reading it to you, you knew the next words before they were spoken. You knew what the next picture would be before someone could turn the page.

God knows us even better than that.

Did you ever have a favorite room and know where everything was in that room—even with your eyes closed? I remember my grandparents' old white house in the little valley like that.

I can close my eyes and hear the old oil stove click-click-clicking as it heated up in the morning. I can see the wooden lamp made by Great-uncle Isaac and the lampshade that was a picture of a lady at a lake. I can see the old white swivel chair that sat in front of the two big windows with a view of the fish pond and the old apple orchard. I can see the little brown desk with the clear, orangey plastic handles and the drawer where Granny kept her list of "odd names" in a brown spiral notebook. I can see the closet where they kept their toys: the red plastic shaver that really buzzed, the jigsaw puzzle of an old mill, and the *Henry the Helicopter* book. I can step out on the front porch and smell the damp forest across the road and hear a quail call through the fog.

I loved that place. So even though the house is just an old wreck now, with sad, empty windows and grass growing up through the front porch, I can see it the way it was.

God loves you and me and knows us that much and more.

He knows everything about you. He could close His eyes right now (but He doesn't need to) and see the way you hold your mouth when you're puzzled about something. He knows what you like to doodle with a pencil. He knows your new favorite color—and all your old favorite colors, too. He's looked into every one of your hiding places. He's visited all of the imaginary places you make up in your mind. He's walked in your dreams. He's felt the disappointments you've felt and never told anyone else.

Now, other people may not understand you at all. You may not even understand yourself sometimes. But there is Someone with you who understands you very, very well.

He *made* you, remember? And nobody loves you more.

O Lord, you have searched me and you know me. You know when I sit and when I rise; you perceive my thoughts from afar. You discern my going out and my lying down; you are familiar with all my ways.

PSALM 139:1–3

HOPE

DICK EASTMAN AND JACK HAYFORD
FROM *LIVING AND PRAYING IN JESUS NAME*

"She'll not live a day," a physician told an attending nurse. Concerned, the nurse befriended the dying woman and in a few hours had won her confidence.

Motioning for the nurse to come near, the old woman said sorrowfully, "I have traveled all the way from California by myself, stopping at every city of importance between San Francisco and Boston. In each city I visit just two places: the police station and the hospital. You see, my boy ran away from home and I have no idea where he is. I've got to find him...."

The mother's eyes seemed to flash a ray of hope as she added, "Someday he may even come into this very hospital, and if he does, please promise me you'll tell him his two best friends never gave up on him...."

Bending over the dying mother, the nurse whispered softly, "Tell me the names of those two friends so I can tell your son if I ever see him."

With trembling lips and her eyes filled with tears the mother responded, "Tell him those two friends were God and his mother," and she closed her eyes and died.

Suppose one of you had a hundred sheep and lost one. Wouldn't you leave the ninety-nine in the wilderness and go after the lost one until you found it? When found, you can be sure you would put it across your shoulders, rejoicing, and when you got home call in your friends and neighbors, saying "Celebrate with me! I've found my lost sheep!" Count on it—there's more joy in heaven over one sinner's rescued life than over ninety-nine good people in no need of rescue.

LUKE 15:3–7, THE MESSAGE

MY GRANDPARENTS' GAME OF LOVE

LAURA JEANNE ALLEN

My grandparents were married for over half a century, and played their own special game from the time they had met each other. The goal of their game was to write the word "shmily" in a surprise place for the other to find. They took turns leaving "shmily" around the house, and as soon as one of them discovered it, it was their turn to hide it once more.

They dragged "shmily" with their fingers through the sugar and flour containers to await whoever was preparing the next meal. They smeared it in the dew on the windows overlooking the patio where my grandma always fed us warm, homemade pudding with blue food coloring. "Shmily" was written in the steam left on the mirror after a hot shower, where it would reappear bath after bath. At one point, my grandmother even unrolled an entire roll of toilet paper to leave "shmily" on the very last sheet.

There was no end to the places "shmily" would pop up. Little notes with "shmily" scribbled hurriedly were found on dashboards and car seats, or taped to steering wheels. The notes were stuffed inside shoes and left under pillows. "Shmily" was written in the dust upon the mantel and traced in the ashes of the fireplace. This mysterious word was as much a part of my grandparents' house as the furniture.

It took me a long time before I was able to fully appreciate my grandparents' game. Skepticism has kept me from believing in true love—one that is pure and enduring. However, I never doubted my grandparents' relationship. They had love down pat. It was more than their flirtatious little games; it was a way of life. Their relationship was based on a devotion and passionate affection which not everyone experiences.

Grandma and Grandpa held hands every chance they could. They stole kisses as they bumped into each other in their tiny kitchen. They finished each other's sentences and shared the daily crossword puzzle and word jumble. My grandma whispered to me about how cute my grandpa was, how handsome and old he had grown to be. She claimed that she really knew "how to pick 'em." Before every meal they bowed their heads and gave thanks, marveling at their blessings: a wonderful family, good fortune, and each other.

But there was a dark cloud in my grandparents' life: my grandmother had breast cancer. The disease had first appeared ten years earlier. As always, Grandpa was with her every step of the way. He comforted her in their yellow room, painted that way so that she could always be surrounded by sunshine, even when she was too sick to go outside.

Now the cancer was again attacking her body. With the help of a cane and my grandfather's steady hand, they went to church every Sunday. But my grandmother grew steadily weaker until, finally, she could not leave the house anymore. For a while, Grandpa would go to church alone, praying to God to watch over his wife. Then one day, what we all dreaded finally happened. Grandma was gone.

"Shmily." It was scrawled in yellow on the pink ribbons of my grandmother's funeral bouquet. As the crowd thinned and the last mourners turned to leave, my aunts, uncles, cousins and other family members came forward and gathered around Grandma one last time. Grandpa stepped up to my grandmother's casket and, taking a shaky breath, he began to sing to her. Through his tears and grief, the song came, a deep and throaty lullaby.

Shaking with my own sorrow, I will never forget that moment. For I knew that, although I couldn't begin to fathom the depth of their love, I had been privileged to witness its unmatched beauty.

S-h-m-i-l-y: See How Much I Love You.

THE ONE THE FATHER LOVES THE MOST

BRENNAN MANNING
FROM *LION AND LAMB*

A professor of mine once told me the following story: "I'm one of thirteen children. One day when I was playing in the street of our hometown, I got thirsty and came into the house for a glass of water. My father had just come home from work to have lunch. He was sitting at the kitchen table with a neighbor. A door separated the kitchen from the pantry and my father didn't know I was there. The neighbor said to my father, 'Joe, there's something I've wanted to ask you for a long time. You have thirteen children. Out of all of them is there one that is your favorite, one you love more than all the others?'"

"I had my ear pressed against the door hoping against hope it would be me. 'That's easy,' my father said. 'That's Mary, the twelve-year-old. She just got braces on her teeth and feels so awkward and embarrassed that she won't go out of the house anymore. Oh, but you asked about my favorite. That's my twenty-three-year-old Peter. His fiancée just broke their engagement, and he is desolate. But the one I really love the most is little Michael. He's totally uncoordinated and terrible in any sport he tries to play. But of course, the apple of my eye is Susan. Only twenty-four, living in her own apartment, and developing a drinking problem. I cry for Susan. But I guess of all the kids...' and my father went on, mentioning

71

each of his thirteen children by name."

The professor ended his story saying: "What I learned was that the one my father loved most was the one who needed him most at that time. And that's the way the Father of Jesus is: he loves those most who need him most, who rely on him, depend upon him, and trust him in everything. Little he cares whether you've been as pure as St. John or as sinful as Mary Magdalene. All that matters is trust. It seems to me that learning how to trust God defines the meaning of Christian living. God doesn't wait until we have our moral life in order before he starts loving us."

Making a Difference

SIGNIFICANCE

If I can stop one heart from breaking, I shall not live in vain.
If I can ease one life the aching, or cool one pain,
Or help one fainting robin into his nest again,
I shall not live in vain.

—EMILY ELIZABETH DICKINSON

THE SOWER

RETOLD BY ALICE GRAY

*T*he tent was packed on that rainy night in Liverpool, England. More than seven hundred had come to worship on the first night of the weeklong meetings. During the singing, the preacher looked out on the crowd and noticed a middle-aged woman whose face seemed to shine with happiness as she sang. When the music ended, the preacher called out to her and said, "Sister, do you have a word for the Lord?"

Without hesitating, she stood to her feet and answered. "Eight years ago I was visiting Sydney, Australia. One day while walking down George Street, an old man in old clothes came up to me and said, 'Excuse me, Ma'am, but may I ask you a question? If you were to die tonight, where would you spend eternity?'"

"For weeks I kept thinking about his question. Finally I contacted a pastor at a church near my home. After talking with him, I started reading the Bible and learning about what it meant to become a Christian. One day I asked Jesus to forgive me for my sins and to come into my life as Lord and Savior. From then until now I have never doubted that when I die, I will spend eternity in heaven."

The second night, an overflow crowd again packed in for the tent meeting. As he had done the night before, the preacher looked out across the sea of new faces. This time he spotted a young man and called out, "Brother, do you have a testimony for the Lord?"

With great enthusiasm the young man stood up and said, "I was stationed in Sydney, Australia during my military service and one day when I was walking downtown, an old man in old clothes came up to me and said, 'Excuse me, sir, may I ask you a question? If you were to die tonight, where would you spend eternity?'"

"Well, that night I couldn't go to sleep as I thought about his question. I remembered things my Christian parents had taught me and stories I had learned in Sunday school. In the early morning hours, I knelt down alongside my bunk and asked Jesus Christ into my life. Every day, I'm more thankful for what He has done for me."

On the third night, the preacher looked out on the crowd—different folks than the nights before. This time he called on a young woman. "Sister, do you have a word for the Lord?"

With a quiet manner and gentle voice, the woman began her story. "Four years ago I was visiting Sydney, Australia." Once again the preacher heard the remarkable story of the old man in old clothes who asked a question. As he listened, the preacher decided he would go to Sydney, Australia, and try to find the old man.

I no longer remember how many days the preacher walked the streets of Sydney, but late one afternoon, an old man in old clothes approached him and said, "Excuse me, sir, may I ask you a question?"

The old man's name was Mr. Jenner, and as they sat together on a bench the preacher told Mr. Jenner about the three testimonies he had heard in Liverpool. The old man started to cry as he listened intently to every detail. With tears coursing down his weathered cheeks, Mr. Jenner finally spoke. "More than ten years ago, I promised God that I would witness to at least one person every day. I never got discouraged, but this is the first I have known that there were people who gave their heart to the Lord. God bless you, sir, for coming."

The Lord promised, some seed will fall on good ground.
SEE MATTHEW 13:8

THE MOST BEAUTIFUL FLOWER

CHERYL L. COSTELLO-FORSHEY

The park bench was deserted as I sat down to read
Beneath the long, straggly branches of an old willow tree.
Disillusioned by life with good reason to frown,
For the world was intent on dragging me down.

And if that weren't enough to ruin my day,
A young boy out of breath approached me, all tired from play.
He stood right before me with his head tilted down
And said with great excitement, "Look what I found!"

In his hand was a flower, and what a pitiful sight,
With its petals all worn—not enough rain, or too little light.
Wanting him to take his dead flower and go off to play,
I faked a small smile and then shifted away.

But instead of retreating he sat next to my side
And placed the flower to his nose
and declared with overacted surprise,
"It sure smells pretty and it's beautiful, too.
That's why I picked it; here, it's for you."

The weed before me was dying or dead.
Not vibrant of colors, orange, yellow or red.
But I knew I must take it, or he might never leave.
So I reached for the flower, and replied, "Just what I need."

But instead of him placing the flower in my hand,
He held it midair without reason or plan.
It was then that I noticed for the very first time
That weed-toting boy could not see: he was blind.

I heard my voice quiver, tears shone like the sun
As I thanked him for picking the very best one.
"You're welcome," he smiled, and then ran off to play,
Unaware of the impact he'd had on my day.

I sat there and wondered how he managed to see
A self-pitying woman beneath an old willow tree.
How did he know of my self-indulged plight?
Perhaps from his heart, he'd been blessed with true sight.

Through the eyes of a blind child, at last I could see
The problem was not with the world; the problem was me.
And for all of those times I myself had been blind,
I vowed to see the beauty in life,
and appreciate every second that's mine.

And then I held that wilted flower up to my nose
And breathed in the fragrance of a beautiful rose
And smiled as I watched that young boy, another weed in his hand
About to change the life of an unsuspecting old man.

*Whatever is true, whatever is noble, whatever is right, whatever is pure,
whatever is lovely, whatever is admirable—
if anything is excellent or praiseworthy—think about such things.*
PHILIPPIANS 4:8

THE DAY I MET DANIEL

RICHARD RYAN

It was an unusually cold day for the month of May. Spring had arrived and everything was alive with color. But a cold front from the north had brought winter's chill back to Indiana.

I sat with two friends in the picture window of a quaint restaurant just off the corner of the town square. The food and the company were both especially good that day. As we talked, my attention was drawn outside, across the street. There, walking into town, was a man who appeared to be carrying all his worldly goods on his back. He was carrying a well-worn sign that read, "I will work for food."

My heart sank. I brought him to the attention of my friends and noticed that others around us had stopped eating to focus on him. Heads moved in a mixture of sadness and disbelief. We continued with our meal, but his image lingered in my mind.

We finished our meal and went our separate ways. I had errands to do and quickly set out to accomplish them. I glanced toward the town square, looking somewhat half-heartedly for the strange visitor. I was fearful, knowing that seeing him again would call for some response.

I drove through town and saw nothing of him. I made some purchases at a store and got back in my car. Deep within me, the spirit of God kept speaking to me: "Don't go back to the office until you've at least driven once more around the square."

And so, with some hesitancy, I headed back into town. As I turned the square's third corner, I saw him. He was standing on the steps of the stone-front church, going through his sack. I stopped and looked, feeling both compelled to speak to him yet wanting to drive on. The empty parking space on the corner seemed to be a sign from God: an invitation to park. I pulled in, got out, and approached the town's newest visitor.

"Looking for the pastor?" I asked.

"Not really," he replied. "Just resting."

"Have you eaten today?"

"Oh, I ate something early this morning."

"Would you like to have lunch with me?"

"Do you have some work I could do for you?"

"No work," I replied. "I commute here to work from the city, but I would like to take you to lunch."

"Sure," he replied with a smile.

As he began to gather his things, I asked some surface questions.

"Where you headed?"

"St. Louis."

"From?"

"Oh, all over; mostly Florida."

"How long you been walking?"

"Fourteen years," came the reply.

I knew I had met someone unusual.

We sat across from each other in the same restaurant I had left only minutes earlier. His hair was long and straight, and he had a neatly trimmed dark beard. His skin was deeply tanned, and his face was weathered slightly beyond his thirty-eight years. His eyes were dark yet clear, and he spoke with eloquence and articulation that was startling. He removed his jacket to reveal a bright red T-shirt that said, "Jesus is The Never Ending Story."

Then Daniel's story began to unfold. He had seen some rough times early in life. He'd made some wrong choices and reaped the consequences.

Fourteen years earlier while backpacking across the country, he had stopped on the beach in Daytona. He tried to hire on with some men who were putting up a large tent and some equipment. A concert, he thought. He was hired, but the tent would house not a concert but revival services, and in those services he would see life more clearly. He gave his life over to God.

"Nothing's been the same since," he said. "I felt the Lord telling me to keep walking, and so I did, some fourteen years now."

"Ever think of stopping?" I asked.

"Oh, once in a while, when it seems to get the best of me. But God has given me this calling. I give out Bibles. That's what's in my pack. I work to buy food and Bibles, and I give them out when his Spirit leads."

I sat amazed. My homeless friend was not homeless. He was on a mission and lived this way by choice. The question burned inside for a moment and then I asked: "What's it like?"

"What?"

"To walk into a town carrying all your things on your back and to show your sign?"

"Oh, it was humiliating at first," Daniel admitted. "People would stare and make comments. Once someone tossed a piece of half-eaten bread at me and made a gesture that certainly didn't make me feel welcome. But then it became humbling to realize that God was using me to touch lives and change peoples' concepts of other folks like me."

My concept was changing, too.

We finished our dessert and gathered his things. Just outside the door he paused. He turned to me and said, "Come ye blessed of my Father and inherit the kingdom I've prepared for you. For when I was hungry you gave me food, and when I was thirsty you gave me drink, a stranger and you took me in."

I felt as if we were on holy ground.

"Could you use another Bible?" I asked. He said he preferred a certain translation. It traveled well and was not too heavy. It was also his personal favorite.

"I've read through it fourteen times," he said.

I was able to find my new friend a Bible that would do well, and he seemed very grateful.

"Where you headed from here?" I asked.

"Well, I found a little map on the back of this amusement park coupon."

"Are you hoping to hire on there for a while?"

"No, I just figure I should go there. I figure someone under that star right there needs a Bible, so that's where I'm going next."

He smiled, and the warmth of his spirit radiated the sincerity of his mission. I drove him back to the town square where we'd met two hours earlier, and as we drove, it began to rain. We parked and unloaded his things.

"Would you sign my autograph book?" he asked. "I like to keep messages from folks I meet."

I wrote in his little book how his commitment to his calling had touched my life. I encouraged him to stay strong. And I left him with a verse of scripture, Jeremiah 29:11. "I know the plans I have for you," declared the Lord, "plans to prosper you and not to harm you. Plans to give you a future and a hope."

"Thanks, man," he said. "I know we just met and we're really just strangers, but I love you."

"I know," I said. "I love you, too."

"The Lord is good."

"Yes, he is. How long has it been since someone hugged you?" I asked.

"A long time," he replied.

And so on the busy street corner in the drizzling rain, my new friend and I embraced, and I felt deep inside that I had been changed.

He put his things on his back, smiled his winning smile, and said, "See you in the New Jerusalem."

"I'll be there!" was my reply.

He began his journey again. He headed away with his sign dangling from his bed roll and pack of Bibles. He stopped, turned and said, "When you see something that makes you think of me, will you pray for me?"

"You bet," I shouted back.

"God Bless."

"God Bless."

And that was the last I saw of him.

Late that evening as I left my office, the wind blew strong. The cold front had settled hard upon the town. I bundled up and hurried to my car. As I sat back and reached for the emergency brake, I saw them—a pair of well-worn brown work gloves neatly laid over the length of the handle. I picked them up and thought of my friend and wondered if his hands would stay warm that night without them. I remembered his request: "If you see something that makes you think of me, will you pray for me?"

Today his gloves lay on my desk in my office. They help me see the world and its people in a new way, and they help me remember those two hours with my unique friend and to pray for his ministry.

"See you in the New Jerusalem," he said.

"Yes, Daniel, I know I will."

THE STATUE

DR. PAUL BRAND AND PHILIP YANCEY
FROM *FEARFULLY AND WONDERFULLY MADE*

After World War II German students volunteered to help rebuild a cathedral in England, one of many casualties of the Luftwaffe bombings. As the work progressed, debate broke out on how to best restore the large statue of Jesus with His arms outstretched and bearing the familiar inscription, "Come unto Me." Careful patching could repair all damage to the statue except for Christ's hands, which had been destroyed by bomb fragments. Should they attempt the delicate task of reshaping those hands?

Finally the workers reached a decision that still stands today. The statue of Jesus has no hands, and the inscription now reads, "Christ has no hands but ours."

Lord, when did we see you hungry and feed you, or thirsty and give you something to drink? When did we see you a stranger and invite you in, or needing clothes and clothe you? When did we see you sick or in prison and go to visit you? The King will reply, "I tell you the truth, whatever you did for one of the least of these brothers of mine, you did for me."

MATTHEW 25:37–40

LIGHT OF THE...
STORAGE CLOSET?

MAX LUCADO

FROM *GOD CAME NEAR*

few nights ago a peculiar thing happened.

An electrical storm caused a blackout in our neighborhood. When the lights went out, I felt my way through the darkness into the storage closet where we keep the candles for nights like this. Through the glow of a lit match I looked up on the shelf where the candles were stored. There they were, already positioned in their stands, melted to various degrees by previous missions. I took my match and lit four of them.

How they illuminated the storage room! What had been a veil of blackness suddenly radiated with soft, golden light! I could see the freezer I had just bumped with my knee. And I could see my tools that needed to be straightened.

"How great it is to have light!" I said out loud, and then spoke to the candles. "If you do such a good job here in the storage closet, just wait till I get you out where you're really needed! I'll put one of you on the table so we can eat. I'll put one of you on my desk so I can read. I'll give one of you to Denalyn so she can cross-stitch. And I'll set you," I took down the largest one, "in the living room where you can light up the whole area." (I felt a bit foolish talking to candles—but what do you do when the lights go out?)

I was turning to leave with the large candle in my hand when I heard a voice, "Now, hold it right there."

I stopped. *Somebody is here!* I thought. Then I relaxed. *It's just Denalyn, teasing me for talking to the candles.*

"OK, honey, cut the kidding," I said in the semidarkness. No answer. *Hmm, maybe it was the wind.* I took another step.

"Hold it, I said!" There was that voice again. My hands began to sweat.

"Who said that?"

"I did." The voice was near my hand.

"Who are you? What are you?"

"I'm a candle." I looked at the candle I was holding. It was burning a strong, golden flame. It was red and sat on a heavy wooden candle holder that had a firm handle.

I looked around once more to see if the voice could be coming from another source. "There's no one here but you, me, and the rest of us candles," the voice informed me.

I lifted up the candle to take a closer look. You won't believe what I saw. There was a tiny face in the wax. (I told you you wouldn't believe me.) Not just a wax face that someone had carved, but a moving, functioning, fleshlike face full of expression and life.

"Don't take me out of here!"

"What?"

"I said, Don't take me out of this room."

"What do you mean? I have to take you out. You're a candle. Your job is to give light. It's dark out there. People are stubbing their toes and walking into walls. You have to come out and light up the place!"

"But you can't take me out. I'm not ready," the candle explained with pleading eyes. "I need more preparation."

I couldn't believe my ears. "More preparation?"

"Yeah, I've decided I need to research this job of light-giving so I won't go out and make a bunch of mistakes. You'd be surprised how distorted the glow of an untrained candle can be. So I'm doing some studying. I just finished a book on wind resistance. I'm in the middle of a great series of tapes on wick build-up and conservation—and I'm reading the new best-seller on flame display. Have you heard of it?"

"No," I answered.

"You might like it. It's called *Waxing Eloquently.*"

"That really sounds inter—" I caught myself. *What am I doing? I'm in here conversing with a candle while my wife and daughters are out there in the darkness!*

"All right then," I said. "You're not the only candle on the shelf. I'll blow you out and take the others!"

But just as I got my cheeks full of air, I heard other voices.

"We aren't going either!"

It was a conspiracy. I turned around and looked at the three other candles; each with flames dancing above a miniature face.

I was beyond feeling awkward about talking to candles. I was getting miffed.

"You are candles and your job is to light dark places!"

"Well, that may be what you think," said the candle on the far left—a long, thin fellow with a goatee and a British accent. "You may think we have to go, but I'm busy."

"Busy?"

"Yes, I'm meditating."

"What? A candle that meditates?"

"Yes. I'm meditating on the importance of light. It's really enlightening."

I decided to reason with them. "Listen, I appreciate what you guys are doing. I'm all for meditation time. And everyone needs to study and research; but for goodness' sake, you guys have been in here for weeks! Haven't you had enough time to get your wick on straight?"

"And you other two," I asked, "are you going to stay in here as well?"

A short, fat, purple candle with plump cheeks that reminded me of Santa Claus spoke up. "I'm waiting to get my life together. I'm not stable enough. I lose my temper easily. I guess you could say that I'm a hothead."

The last candle had a female voice, very pleasant to the ear. "I'd like to help," she explained, "but lighting the darkness is not my gift."

All this was sounding too familiar. "Not your gift? What do you mean?"

"Well, I'm a singer. I sing to other candles to encourage them to burn more brightly." Without asking my permission, she began a rendition of "This Little Light of Mine." (I have to admit, she had a good voice.)

The other three joined in, filling the storage room with singing.

"Hey," I shouted above the music, "I don't mind if you sing while you work! In fact, we could use a little music out there!"

They didn't hear me. They were singing too loudly. I yelled louder.

"Come on, you guys. There's plenty of time for this later. We've got a crisis on our hands."

They wouldn't stop. I put the big candle on the shelf and took a step back and considered the absurdity of it all. Four perfectly healthy candles singing to each other about light but refusing to come out of the closet. I had all I could take. One by one I blew them out. They kept singing to the end. The last one to flicker was the female. I snuffed her out right in the "puff" part of "Won't let Satan puff me out."

I stuck my hands in my pockets and walked back out in the darkness. I bumped my knee on the same freezer. Then I bumped into my wife.

"Where are the candles?" she asked.

"They don't…they won't work. Where did you buy those candles anyway?"

"Oh, they're church candles. Remember the church that closed down across town? I bought them there."

I understood.

Let your light shine before men, that they may see your good deeds
and praise your Father in heaven.
MATTHEW 5:16

NURTURING ACROSS THE GENERATIONS

JUDY A. WAGNER

When I was married at the tender age of nineteen, I thought I knew all about marriage and raising a family. But it was my mother-in-law who patiently taught me the subtle art of becoming a woman.

She was fifty-five years old when I became part of her family. For nearly thirty-five years my husband and I have lived next door to his parents on the farm where his mother grew up. We share a unique relationship that few couples can understand in this modern, fast-paced world. No need for traveling or telephoning to keep in touch. Every day our lives intermingled as we shared our joys and struggles on the family farm.

After a long day of weeding or training berries, she'd invite her son and me in for supper. "I've got a pot roast going with carrots and spuds," she'd say. "You guys can have some if you'd like." Afterwards she and I would clean up the dishes in her big farm kitchen, and discuss how to cook a beef roast to keep it moist, or how to preserve carrots from the garden by burying them in a bucket of wood shavings.

Some days when the work was caught up, we'd hurry off to town to run errands for the men and still manage to squeeze in a little shopping. We took sewing classes together and often critiqued each other's homemade clothes. "Looks like Lady Aster's horse, doesn't it?" she'd say grinning as she'd anxiously model one of her outfits for me, and then we'd both laugh and continue to encourage one another.

As the years grew so did the special bond between us. She excelled at being a good listener and used her arms often for hugs. She deeply sympathized and prayed with me during the years I desperately struggled to have children, and rejoiced with me at the birth of our first child.

Somehow all the yesterdays just quietly slipped away. One day when she was nearing her eightieth birthday, I noticed she was somewhat confused and disoriented. It was all so subtle at first. We hardly even noticed that Alzheimer's had gradually begun to steal her mind away.

Now, in her late eighties, she can't remember the seasons of the year, holidays, and the visits of family members. Her anxious hands no longer accomplish the old, familiar chores that her heart remembers. Some days she doesn't know her devoted husband and is fearful of the strange man in her house. Frightened, she often comes to see me.

"Oh, thank you, sweetie," she says with wide, moist eyes. "You're just like having a big sister. I feel so much better now. I know I can always count on you."

I don't understand why she must endure this dreadful illness, yet somehow I realize that God is very near, for I see his reflection in her loving eyes. My heart aches for her, and even though I can't change what is happening, I'll be there for her and love her through it. I've learned how to do this well because I've had such a wonderful teacher.

Let the older women teach the younger.
SEE TITUS 2:4

THE QUARTER THAT BOUGHT A PASTOR

L. DOWARD MCBAIN

FROM *LEADERSHIP JOURNAL*

In a tiny Colorado church where my new wife and I were serving one summer, Mrs. Rolf was one of four devout parishioners who met for prayer each Thursday afternoon. She rarely missed.

She lived with her twelve-year-old son, who was spending the summer herding sheep to buy school clothes for the coming fall. Mrs. Rolf's husband had left her several years earlier for reasons that never seemed clear. She was destitute and received meager relief from the community.

Before we knew it, the summer was gone; our last weekend had come. Saturday night the congregation threw us a farewell party. They brought many practical gifts for the young couple returning to seminary in Philadelphia—kitchen utensils and enough canned goods to last many weeks. But Mrs. Rolf wasn't there.

The next morning the little church was packed for my farewell sermon, but our special friend was missing again. So, shortly after the service, we finished our packing, bagged some extra groceries, and drove out to see Mrs. Rolf.

She answered my knock by a feeble call from her bed. She explained that she was too weak to get up, and regretted not being able to attend our party or the last worship service. She then hinted she was partly relieved because she had no gift to give the minister and his wife. She asked me to pray for her son.

Then before I left she said she remembered she did have something to give. Would I promise to take it? Not being able to refuse her I said yes. She told me where to find it, and I nervously moved to the other room—the only other room in the house.

There was a small table with two chairs, a little potbelly stove and a new lid-lifter she said the relief board had given her the previous week. Her gift was on the top ledge, she said. She must be wrong. But, to be sure, I reached to the far right and slowly brought my hand back across the empty board until I quickly knew that she was right. There it was: a quarter.

I took it to her and said I could not accept it. She reminded me of my promise. "You must take it. It is all I have to give." I protested, but I took it.

Her last words to me were enough for a lifetime. "Use it as you go back to seminary and prepare to be a good minister of God."

I do not know what happened to that twenty-five cents. I only know what happened to me. In many ways that quarter bought a minister. More than fifty years later, I have never been able to shake off this godly woman's sacrifice.

This poor widow has put more into the treasury than all the others. They all gave out of their wealth; but she, out of her poverty, put in everything—all she had to live on.
MARK 12:43–44

LOVE THAT BLOSSOMS

NANETTE THORSEN-SNIPES
FROM *WOMAN'S TOUCH*

Curiously, the warmth of the spring day felt good on my skin. I fought back the veil of tears that blurred the dogwood trees lining the hospital grounds. Everything around me seemed to be bursting with life while I felt cold, alone and defeated.

With a sinking feeling, I opened my car door and drove to the florist. I knew I had to do this for my mother. She had always said, "Give me flowers while I can enjoy them."

As I opened the door to the florist's shop, I was met by a profusion of color mingled with the scent of fresh roses. What a contrast with the bare hospital room I had just left!

My mother had been in the hospital for more than two weeks, her year-long struggle with lung cancer nearly at an end. I wanted more than anything to see her smile once more.

I walked between the potted daisies, pausing to finger the petals. They still shimmered with water droplets, and I couldn't help thinking how vibrant they seemed. The shelves below them were lined with dish gardens exploding with philodendron. Everything seemed blessed with the fullness of life and the will to live.

I turned and faced the sunlight streaming through the window, hoping it would drive out the ache in my throat. I breathed in deeply, then glanced up at the top shelf. There I saw an old-fashioned yellow sprinkling can brimming with lavender daisies. As I lifted it from the shelf, the flowers practically danced.

"Could I help you?" a voice behind me asked.

I turned to face a woman I didn't know. She must have sensed the pain in my heart or seen the tears in my eyes because her eyes were full of compassion.

"I-I want something pretty for my mother," I managed to say. "She is dying." Without so much as a word, the woman who worked daily nurturing life with the flower shop walked forward. Her deep brown eyes melted into a mixture of pain, understanding, and love as she gently placed her arms around me.

In that unexpected embrace, I felt God's love as He welcomed me into His arms, surrounding and protecting me from the pain. At once, the familiar words of Jesus spoke clearly to me, "By this shall all men know that ye are my disciples, if ye have love one to another" (John 13:35, KJV).

There in that flower shop, God met me, a defeated and lonely person trying to muddle through a tragedy without Him. But through His love, He sent someone to meet me in my sorrow.

I thank God every day for this woman who allowed the love of Jesus to work through her. My prayer is that I follow her example and meet others where they are, freely offering the love of Jesus.

SWEET FRAGRANCE

MICHAEL P. GREEN
FROM *ILLUSTRATIONS FOR BIBLICAL PREACHING*

*T*he story has been told of a missionary to China who was in language school. The very first day of class the teacher entered the room and, without saying a word, walked down every row of students. Finally, still without saying a word, she walked out of the room again. Then she came back and addressed the class.

"Did you notice anything special about me?" she asked. Nobody could think of anything in particular. One student finally raised her hand. "I noticed that you had on a very lovely perfume," she said. The class chuckled. But the teacher said, "That was exactly the point. You see, it will be a long time before any of you will be able to speak Chinese well enough to share the Gospel with anyone in China. But even before you are able to do that, you can minister the sweet fragrance of Christ to these people by the quality of your lives. It is your lifestyle, lived out among the Chinese people, that will minister Christ to them long before you are able to say one word to them about personal faith in Jesus."

As far as God is concerned there is a sweet, wholesome
fragrance in our lives. It is the fragrance of Christ within us,
an aroma to both the saved and the unsaved all around us.
2 CORINTHIANS 2:15, *THE LIVING BIBLE*

MINISTRY WOMAN

Robin Jones Gunn

had a moment in my life, as we all do, when a bit of eternal truth broke through my "convenient Christianity," and I was radically changed.

We lived in a small university town where God opened up many opportunities for ministry. My husband was working as a youth pastor. We had teenagers over to our house all the time and even had a college student living with us. I accepted a part-time position as what they called a "radio personality" at a Christian station in town. I was busy writing a series of teen novels for a Christian publisher, and women's groups were calling and asking me to speak at various events. In every way, I was Ministry Woman!

One night I was on the phone with my best friend, Donna. In three weeks she and I were flying to Europe where I'd been invited to speak. There was so much to do, and I told Donna, "If one more person asks for one more little piece of me, I'm going to fall apart! I have no more pieces left to give."

As I was speaking to her, the call waiting signal on my phone started beeping. I ignored it but the caller continued to dial in. "Just a minute, Donna."

It was almost ten o'clock, and the caller turned out to be my neighbor, Jana. She said, "Robin, I didn't know who else to call...could you come up? Just for a minute?"

I thought, *Okay. This is it. The last piece of my sanity and now my neighbor wants to take it from me. Doesn't it ever let up?*

I considered saying no. I thought she would certainly understand if I said it was too late. I would come see her in the morning. Whatever it was could wait until then, couldn't it?

"Oh, all right," I heard myself tell Jana. "I'll be there in a minute."

I told Donna I'd have to call her back, and I jerked the front door open ready to march up the street to Jana's house.

It was a crisp, cold night. It had been snowing. That, and the fact that I walked out without a jacket made me feel even more inconvenienced. I couldn't imagine what Jana wanted. I'd invited her to church with me, but she hadn't come. I'd given her all my books, but she hadn't read them. I'd told her when my radio program aired, but she never listened. I'd given her two books by important Christian psychologists when her husband left her, but she hadn't gotten around to reading them. The way I saw it, I'd done my part. Jana simply wasn't interested in coming to the Lord.

When I arrived at her front door, Jana stood there on crutches.

I'd forgotten that she told me a week ago that she was having her right hip replaced. She had now had both hips replaced before she was thirty-five due to arthritis. I knew her mom had come from the East Coast the first few days to help out. Her ex-husband had their two daughters every Thursday, and this was Thursday. Her mom had gone home, and Jana stood before me, all alone.

"Thanks so much for coming," Jana said showing me in and hobbling to the hospital bed set up in the family room. "I didn't know who else to call. You see, I wanted to go to bed, but..." she looked down at her feet. "I couldn't take off my shoes."

In that moment, I realized that I thought I was "ministry woman," and yet I was not worthy to untie the laces on my neighbor's tennis shoes.

I knelt down, and let me tell you, it was all I could do to not wash her feet with my tears. I saw what God desired of my life. I suddenly understood His concept of ministry. All God has asked me to do is to love Him and love my neighbor.

That's what a real ministry woman does.

I untied Jana's shoes and slipped them off her feet. Then I helped her take off her sweat pants. I saw the scar. It was vile. *So much pain,* I thought. *And no one here to comfort you.*

Jana slid into bed but I didn't want to leave just because my task was done. I pulled the comforter up to her chin and asked if she'd like a cup of cold water.

I brought one for her. *In Jesus' name,* I thought, as she sipped from the glass tumbler.

Then before I could be self-conscious about what she might think of me, I kissed her on the cheek and said, "Good night, Jana. I love you."

"I know," she said. "That's why I called you. I knew you would come."

A year and a half later, Jana gave her life to the Lord. We had moved to another state when she told me her good news on the phone. She was excited about plans to go on the woman's retreat and the weekly Bible study group at the church she was attending.

More than once I have wondered what would have happened if I had said no on that snowy night. After all, I had books to write, planes to catch, and a radio show to record in the morning. What if I had missed the opportunity for the pure and undefiled ministry of loving my neighbor simply because I was too caught up in my own version of being Ministry Woman?

I Wonder

You know, Lord, how I serve You
With great emotional fervor
In the limelight.
You know how eagerly I speak for You
At the women's club.
You know how I effervesce when I promote
A fellowship group.
You know my genuine enthusiasm
At a Bible study.

But how would I react, I wonder,
If you pointed to a basin of water
And asked me to wash the calloused feet
Of a bent and wrinkled old woman
Day after day
Month after month
In a room where nobody saw
And nobody knew.

—RUTH HARMS CALKIN,
FROM TELL ME AGAIN, LORD, I FORGET

UNANSWERED LETTERS

AUTHOR UNKNOWN

I read of a man who was involved in a tragic accident. He lost both legs and his left arm and only a finger and thumb remained on the right hand. But he still possessed a brilliant mind, enriched with a good education and broadened with world travel. At first he thought there was nothing he could do but remain a helpless sufferer.

A thought came to him. It was always nice to receive letters, but why not write them—he could still use his right hand with some difficulty. But to whom could he write?

Was there anyone shut in and incapacitated like he was who could be encouraged by his letters? He thought of men in prison—they did have some hope of release whereas he had none—but it was worth a try.

He wrote to a Christian organization concerned with prison ministry. He was told that his letters could not be answered—it was against prison rules, but he commenced this one-sided correspondence.

He wrote twice a week, and it taxed his strength to the limit. But into the letters he put his whole soul, all his experience, all his faith, all his wit, and all his Christian optimism. Frequently he felt discouraged and was tempted to give it up. But it was his one remaining activity, and he resolved to continue as long as he could.

At last he got a letter. It was very short, written on prison stationery by the officer whose duty it was to censor the mail. All it said was: "Please write on the best paper you can afford. Your letters are passed from cell to cell till they literally fall to pieces."

No matter what our personal situation is, we still have God-given gifts and talents, experience, and encouragement that we can share with others.

God has given each of you some special abilities; be sure to use them to help each other, passing on to others God's many kinds of blessings.

1 PETER 4:10, *THE LIVING BIBLE*

Changed Lives

MENDING

Man is broken. He lives by mending.
The grace of God is glue.

—Eugene O'Neill

HOW SWEET THE SOUND

CYNTHIA HAMOND

$\mathcal{T}$he lead should have been mine. All my friends agreed with me. At least, it shouldn't have been Helen's, that strange new girl. She never had a word to say, always looking down at her feet as if her life was too heavy to bear. What's up with that anyway? We've never done anything to her. We think she's just stuck up. Things can't be all that bad for her, not with all the great clothes she wears. She hasn't worn the same thing more then twice in the two months she's been at our school.

But the worst of it was when she showed up at our tryouts and sang for my part. Everyone knew the lead role was meant for me. After all, I had parts in all our high school musicals and this was our senior year.

My friends were waiting for me, so I didn't hang around for Helen's audition. The shock came two days later when we hurried to check the drama department's bulletin board for the play postings.

We scanned the sheets looking for my name. When we found it, I burst out in tears. Helen was slated to play the lead! I was to be her mother and her understudy. Understudy? Nobody could believe it.

Rehearsals seemed to go on forever. Helen didn't seem to notice that we were going out of our way to ignore her.

I'll admit it, Helen did have a beautiful voice. She was different on stage somehow. Not so much happy as settled and content.

Opening night had all its jitters. Everyone was quietly bustling around backstage waiting for the curtain to go up. Everyone but Helen, of course. She seemed contained in her own calm world.

The performance was a hit. Our timing was perfect; our voices blended and soared. Helen and I flowed back and forth, weaving the story between us. I, the ailing mother praying for her wayward daughter and Helen, playing the daughter, who realizes as her mother dies that there is more to this life than *this* life.

The final scene reached its dramatic end. I was laying in the darkened bedroom. The prop bed I was on was uncomfortable, making it hard to stay still. I was impatient, anxious for Helen's big finish to be over.

She was spotlighted upstage, the grieving daughter beginning to understand the true meaning of the hymn she had been singing as her mother passed away.

"Amazing Grace, how sweet the sound...." Her voice lifted over the pain of her mother's death and the joy of God's promises.

"...that saved a wretch like me..." Something real was happening to me as Helen sang. My impatience left.

"...I once was lost but now I am found..." My heart was touched to tears.

"...was blind but now I see." My spirit began to turn within me, and I turned to God. In that moment, I knew His love, His desire for me.

Helen's voice lingered in the prayer of the last note. The curtain dropped.

Complete silence. Not a sound. Helen stood behind the closed curtain, head bowed, gently weeping.

Suddenly applause and cheers erupted, and when the curtain parted, Helen saw her standing ovation.

We all made our final bows. My hugs were genuine. My heart had been opened to the Great Love.

Then it was over. The costumes were hung up, makeup tissued off, the lights dimmed. Everyone went off in their usual groupings, congratulating each other.

Everyone but Helen. And everyone but me.

"Helen, your song, it was so real for me." I hesitated, my feelings intense. "You sang me into the heart of God."

Helen gasped. Her eyes met mine.

"That's what my mother said to me the night she died." A tear slipped down her cheek. My heart leapt to hers. "My mother was in such pain. Singing 'Amazing Grace' always comforted her. She said I should always remember that God has promised good to me and that His grace would lead her home."

Her face lit from the inside out, her mother's love shining through. "Just before she died she whispered, 'Sing me into the heart of God, Helen.' That night and tonight, I sang for my mother."

ELLIE AND ROLF

REBECCA MANLEY PIPPERT
FROM *A HEART LIKE HIS*

Throughout history God's people have been willing to pay the price for truth and loyalty. A gray-haired woman of sixty with a heavy German accent spoke to a congregation in Tennessee. She was a Jew who had been captured as a teenager and sent to prison camp during the second world war. Her story was not unlike others of the tragic suffering of prisoners inside German concentration camps.

After months of abuse and malnutrition that led to starvation, she realized that if she had any hope of escaping she had to do it while she still had some strength. Having just graduated from high school, she saw women just a few years older than she was who already looked elderly. She plotted an escape carefully, and tried to leave no detail to chance.

On the night of her escape she had maneuvered every challenge successfully. There was only one hurdle left—a literal one. She had to scale a barbed wire fence to get outside the compound. She was halfway up the fence when the S.S. guard on duty spotted her. He screamed for her to stop, and at gunpoint demanded that she drop down. She did, her knees and legs badly bleeding. She began sobbing, realizing that her only hope of escape had just vanished.

But to her astonishment she heard the guard say, "Ellie? Is that you? It can't be possible!" She looked into his face and realized it was Rolf, a fellow classmate who had been her best friend in middle school. They had shared so many secret dreams and aspirations then. But now it was wartime, and they were on opposite sides. "Oh, Rolf, go ahead and kill me. Please! I have no reason to live. I have lost all hope. Get it over with and let me die now. There's nothing to live for anyway."

"Ellie, you are so wrong. There is everything to live for so long as you know *who* to live for. I'm going to let you go. I'll guard you until you climb the wall and get on the other side. But would you promise me one thing?"

Ellie looked at him incredulously, thinking he must be joking, but she could see his intensity and knew he meant every word. "What is it, Rolf?" she asked.

"Promise me when you get on the other side and become free, that you will ask one question continuously until someone answers it for you. Ask, 'Why does Jesus Christ make life worth living?' Promise me, Ellie! He's the only reason to live. Promise me you'll ask until you get the answer."

"Yes, I promise, I promise!" she shouted. As she furiously climbed the fence she felt guilty. *I would have said anything,* she thought to herself, *to get out of this hellhole.*

As she dropped to the other side into freedom, she heard several deafening shots. She turned to look as she ran, convinced that Rolf had changed his mind and amazed that his bullets had missed. To her horror, she saw that other S.S. guards, having realized that Rolf allowed and aided her escape, had killed him on the spot. It was as she ran to her freedom that it dawned on her that Rolf died for her that she might know this Jesus. She wondered who this Jesus Christ was, that someone would lay down his own life so that she could know him.

At just the right time, when we were still powerless, Christ died for the ungodly. Very rarely will anyone die for a righteous man, though for a good man someone might possibly dare to die. But God demonstrates his own love for us in this: While we were still sinners, Christ died for us.

ROMANS 5:6–8

Fanfare

Quietly
He called me
Humanly speaking
it was no extravaganza;
earth scarcely noticed
Yet I've been told
that beyond the galaxies
a fanfare broke out
when I said 'Yes' to Him
and took His Name.

—NANCY SPIEGELBERG
FROM *FANFARE*

NEW MAN

J. G.

FROM *SONS: A FATHER'S LOVE*

When my son Scott called and asked to talk to me, I didn't want to take the call. My wife, our other children, and I had been through years of ups and downs with him and his drug abuse. We'd heard a thousand promises and seen them broken twice as many times. Scott had stolen from us, manipulated us, and failed us. He had broken my wife's heart and turned my optimism into cynicism. It had been a relief not to hear from him for two years. Now he was on the phone, and he was just about the last person on earth I wanted to hear from.

"Get his number and tell him I'll call him back," I told my secretary, wanting time to think. When I saw the area code, I realized that Scott was in a different state, and my curiosity was stirred. When I finally got myself psyched up to place the call, I was surprised when the woman who answered said, "Oakridge Christian Center."

"Could I speak to Scott Granger, please?"

"Who's calling?"

"His father, returning his call." There was a brief pause, and then I heard Scott's voice.

"Hi, Dad. Thanks for calling me back."

So began the most amazing phone conversation I've ever had. Scott told me that he had been through another rehab program a year and a half ago, but this one had provided something no other program had offered. "I met Jesus Christ," he explained.

"What does that mean?" I asked, wondering if he'd really lost his mind this time.

"It means that I've been forgiven for my past, that Jesus died for all my sins, and that He's given me a new life. And I want to ask you and Mom to forgive me, too. I'm born again, Dad. I'm a new man."

He went on to tell me that he was actually working for the church, helping other addicts get their lives straightened out. I was speechless; torn between the hope that he was really straightened out this time, fearful that he had become some kind of a religious fanatic, and cynical with the cold, bitter thought, *Right. Here we go again.*

The young man who arrived at the airport two weeks later looked like a stranger to me. He was well groomed and nicely dressed, and his eyes were bright and clear. He was probably as nervous as I was, but he quickly and spontaneously took his mother in his arms, and they both began to cry. I was braced for deception, but there was an undeniable difference in this initial meeting.

In the days that followed, Scott told us his story. In the midst of drug withdrawal, he had seen a vision of Jesus Christ on the cross and had cried out to Him for help. His withdrawal symptoms had ended instantly, and the experience had led him to a church. "I asked Jesus to be my Lord," he quietly explained. "And my life has never been the same since."

My wife and I had never really been churchgoers, but the change in Scott was too dramatic to ignore. And when he showed us the story in the New Testament about the prodigal son, we discovered that just as we had welcomed Scott home, God was waiting with open arms to welcome us home, too. Today, ten years later, our family is a Christian family. Jesus has taught us about forgiveness, new life, and renewed hope. He has given us back the son we had lost.

And He has given us the same new life He gave to our prodigal son.

The son said to him, "Father I have sinned against heaven
and against you. I am no longer worthy to be called
your son." But the father said to his servants, "Quick!
Bring the best robe and put it on him. Put a ring on
his finger and sandals on his feet. Bring the fatted calf
and kill it. Let's have a feast and celebrate. For this son
of mine was dead and is alive again; he was lost and is found."

LUKE 15:21–24

Along the Road

I walked a mile with Pleasure;
She chattered all the way,
But left me none the wiser
For all she had to say.
I walked a mile with Sorrow
And ne'er a word said she;
But oh, the things I learned from her
When Sorrow walked with me!

—ROBERT BROWNING HAMILTON

GOD HAS A PLAN
FOR YOUR BABY

NANCY SULLIVAN GENG

The hospital room was wrapped in early morning darkness as bright flakes of November snow fell outside the window near my bed. My husband slept soundly on a cot that the nurses had set up, but I drifted in and out of restless sleep.

I kept recounting the previous night in fragments: labor…pain…a baby…a diagnosis.

Then slowly opening my eyes, I remembered the doctor's midnight words: "I'm sorry, Mr. and Mrs. Geng…. Our preliminary findings indicate that your baby has the symptoms and tendencies of Down syndrome."

The digital clock on top of my suitcase clicked to 6:02 A.M. I was worn and tired. I wanted to sleep but unanswerable questions kept me from rest:

What did the future hold?

How would we tell our families?

Would our marriage adjust to the ongoing challenges of her disability?

Then, I heard a soft knocking sound. Turning my glance to the door I saw the silhouette of a young ponytailed girl in a pleated skirt, her outline shadowed by the dim lights of the hospital hallway.

As she moved closer, I brushed the sleep from my eyes to make out the face. It was Jessy. We smiled, simultaneously. As she sat down in a chair next to my bed, I called to mind memories from a September morning just the year before. I was newly graduated from college; it was the first day of my teaching career.

I had been assigned to Room 202, in a Catholic high school.

As the school bell sounded through the aging brick corridors, twenty-one sophomores entered my 8:00 A.M. homeroom, a fifteen-minute block of time that preceded scheduled classes, a time reserved for announcements and attendance.

The students were all girls, all uniformed in the black woolen pleats and white starched collars of an eighty-year tradition. Carrying backpacks weighted with college prep books, they squeaked to their desks in polished saddle shoes.

"I'm Mrs. Geng," I announced as I wrote my name on the blackboard.

Jessy, along with the other girls in the class, watched closely and whispered. I, too, was uniformed, but I knew that my navy blue tweeds and professional pumps could not conceal my youth and inexperience.

But as the mornings passed, those homeroom whispers found a voice in the brief conversations we began to exchange.

Sometimes we talked of academic pressures.

Other times, our topics were more lighthearted, especially on Monday morning when the girls bantered about the weekend: basketball games and slumber parties, dances and dresses and dates.

But somehow it always seemed that those homeroom conversations flowed into curious questions about my life:

Was the college I attended a good one?

What was my first date like?

How did I meet my young husband?

I never grew tired of their inquiries or sharing my life with them. They were like younger sisters eager for advice and insight. And though my college professors had warned against becoming "too friendly" with the students, I was honored to offer what little I had learned about life.

The year passed quickly. Then one spring morning in May, I came to homeroom clutching an ultrasound picture I had gotten from the doctor just a day earlier.

Revealing that I was three months pregnant, the girls cheered and began kidding me about maternity clothes and support hose. They agreed unanimously that surely it would be a girl.

Then as they gathered around my desk, I uncreased the black and white sonogram as I outlined the baby's heart and head and hands. The girls looked on in wonder and amazement, all except Jessy. She stood back from the group, her blond ponytailed hair framing a somber smile and blue eyes that hinted of secret sadness.

As homeroom ended with the sound of a bell, the girls rushed off to their first hour classes, but Jessy lingered behind.

"Mrs. Geng...can I talk to you?" she asked in almost a whisper.

"Sure," I said as I glanced at my teaching schedule; I was free until nine o'clock. We sat down in side-by-side desks.

"I'm pregnant, too," she began, her eyes now welling up with tears.

"I'm almost four months along, and I don't know what to do.... My mom is divorced. She's worked hard to afford my tuition.... How am I going to tell her? What will she say? What will she do if I can't stay in school?"

For a moment, Jessy just covered her face with her hands.

"It's okay, Jessy...tell me more," I said.

When she gained her composure, she talked about the child's father, a star football player from the boys' school across the street.

"He's been nominated for an athletic scholarship.... We both know we're too young to get married, too young to take care of a baby.... I'm so scared, Mrs. Geng."

As I listened, I wasn't sure if she could receive the words I felt compelled to say, but I offered them nonetheless:

"Jessy," I began. "God has a plan for your baby. Don't ever forget that." As the last days of school approached, Jessy and I met often to talk.

During that time, Jessy told her mom about the pregnancy and found unforeseen compassion and comfort along with a loving coach to support her through birthing classes.

I, in turn, met with the principal to strategize how we as a school might help Jessy and her family during the remaining months of her pregnancy.

Much to Jessy's surprise, the school invited her to return to classes in the fall, even though her due date was scheduled for mid October, just six weeks before mine.

All through the summer months, I thought of Jessy as I gathered gifts at baby showers and when I shopped for car seats and crib sheets and bumper pads.

Every time I felt the motions and movements of my baby, I couldn't help but visualize her meeting with social workers and signing adoption policies and paging through biographies of prospective parents.

Her plans and preparations for birth were so much different than mine....

When the autumn days of early September arrived, Jessy greeted me in the doorway of Room 202. Wearing a plaid maternity top, blue jeans, and tennis shoes, she waved her class schedule and called out with a smile: "I'm in your homeroom again, Mrs. Geng!"

We tried to hug each other but found it impossible. After almost eight months of pregnancy, our stomachs were the same size. We laughed.

Four weeks later, Jessy delivered a healthy baby girl. After just a few days of recovery, she was back in homeroom neatly uniformed. There she showed me pictures of the baby she had given away, the daughter she had cradled in the hospital for a few short hours.

"I told her that I loved her, Mrs. Geng...."

Now, as the first snow of the season fell outside my hospital window, I, too, had given birth. Jessy had come to visit, to welcome my Down syndrome daughter.

She had come in the early morning hours, before school, to offer me the words I had once offered her:

"Mrs. Geng," she began. "God has a plan for your baby. Don't ever forget that...."

I looked at her and smiled.

For so many months I had felt compelled to teach her to trust in God's plan. How well she had learned that lesson. She knew it by heart.

Now trust was the tender lesson she could teach me.

It's been twelve years since that day. Just a few weeks back as I waited in my car at a corner stoplight, Jessy pulled up right next to me in a station wagon.

I waved. She honked.

There was a baby sleeping right next to her in a car seat. When the light changed, Jessy drove away, but my Down syndrome daughter and her two younger sisters called out from the backseat, "Who was that, Mommy?"

I smiled.

"That was a teacher I once knew, one of my best."

"For I know the plans I have for you," declares the Lord,
"plans to prosper you and not to harm you,
plans to give you hope and a future."

JEREMIAH 29:11

THAT'S MY DADDY

STEVEN J. LAWSON
FROM *THE LEGACY*

A little girl was once standing on the edge of a crowd while her daddy was giving a testimony about what Jesus Christ had done in his life. He was testifying how the Lord had saved him and delivered him from his old lifestyle as a drunkard.

There was a cynic standing on the edge of the crowd that day who could not bear to hear anymore of this religious nonsense. So he yelled, "Why don't you shut up and sit down, old man. You're just *dreaming.*"

Soon, this skeptic felt a tug on his coat sleeve. He looked down and it was this little girl. She looked him square in the eyes and said, "Sir, that's my daddy you're talking about. You say that my daddy is a dreamer? Let me tell you about my daddy.

"My daddy used to be a drunkard and would come home at night and beat my mother. She would cry all through the night. And mister, we didn't have good clothes to wear because my daddy spent all his money on whiskey. Sometimes I didn't even have shoes to wear to school. But look at these shoes and look at this dress! My daddy has a good job now."

Then pointing across the way, she said, "Do you see that woman smiling over there? That's my mother. She doesn't cry through the night anymore. Now she sings."

Then the knockout punch. She said, "Jesus has changed my daddy. Jesus has changed our home. Mister, if my daddy is dreaming, *please don't wake him up.*"

THE MATCHLESS PEARL

AUTHOR UNKNOWN

David Morse—American missionary to India—became great friends there with the pearl-diver, Rambhau. Many an evening he spent in Rambhau's cabin reading to him from the Bible and explaining to him God's way of salvation.

Rambhau enjoyed listening to the Word of God, but whenever the missionary tried to get Rambhau to accept Christ as his Savior, he would shake his head and reply, "Your Christian way to heaven is too easy for me! I cannot accept it. If ever I should find admittance to heaven in that manner, I would feel like a pauper there, like a beggar who has been let in out of pity. I may be proud—but I want to deserve, I want to earn my place in heaven—and so I am going to work for it."

Nothing the missionary could say seemed to have any effect on Rambhau's decision, and so quite a few years slipped by. One evening, however, the missionary heard a knock on his door, and on going to open it he found Rambhau there.

"Come in, dear friend," said Morse.

"No," said the pearl-diver. "I want you to come with me to my house, Sahib, for a short time—I have something to show you. Please do not say No.

"Of course I'll come," replied the missionary. As they neared his house, Rambhau said: "In a week's time I start working for my place in heaven; I am leaving for Delhi—and I am going there on my knees."

STORIES FOR A FAITHFUL HEART

"Man, you're crazy! It's nine hundred miles to Delhi, and the skin will break on your knees, and you will have blood-poisoning or leprosy before you get to Bombay."

"No, I must get to Delhi," affirmed Rambhau, "and the immortals will reward me for it! The suffering will be sweet—for it will purchase heaven for me!"

"Rambhau, my friend—you can't. How can I bear you to do it when Jesus Christ has suffered and died to purchase heaven for you!"

But the old man could not be moved. "You are my dearest friend on earth, Sahib Morse. Through all these years you have stood by me in sickness, in want. You have been sometimes my only friend. But even you cannot turn me from my desire to purchase eternal bliss…. I must go to Delhi!"

Inside the hut, Morse was seated in the very chair Rambhau had specially built for him—where on so many occasions he had read to him the Bible.

Rambhau left the room to return soon with a small but heavy English strongbox. "I have had this box for years," said he, "and I keep only one thing in it. Now I will tell you about it, Sahib Morse. I once had a son…"

"A son! Why, Rambhau, you have never before said a word about him!"

"No, Sahib, I couldn't." Even as he spoke the diver's eyes were moistened.

"Now I must tell you, for soon I will leave, and who knows whether I shall ever return? My son was a diver, too. He was the best pearl diver on the coasts of India. He had the swiftest dive, the keenest eye, the strongest arm, the longest breath of any man who ever sought for pearls.

"What joy he brought to me! Most pearls, as you know, have some defect or blemish only the expert can discern, but my boy always dreamed of finding the 'perfect' pearl—one beyond all that was ever found. One day he found it! But even when he saw it—he had been under water too long…. That pearl cost him his life, for he died soon after."

The old pearl diver bowed his head. For a moment his whole body shook, but there was no sound. "All these years," he continued, "I have kept this pearl, but now I am going, not to return, and to you, my best friend, I am giving my pearl."

The old man worked the combination on the strongbox and drew from it a carefully wrapped package. Gently opening the cotton, he picked up a mammoth pearl and placed it in the hand of the missionary.

It was one of the largest pearls ever found off the coast of India and glowed with a luster and brilliance never seen in cultured pearls. It would have brought a fabulous sum in any market.

For a moment the missionary was speechless and gazed with awe. "Rambhau! What a pearl!"

"That pearl, Sahib, is perfect," replied the Indian quietly. The missionary looked up quickly with a new thought: Was not this the very opportunity and occasion he had prayed for—to make Rambhau understand the value of Christ's sacrifice? So he said, designedly, "Rambhau, this is a wonderful pearl, an amazing pearl. Let me buy it. I would give you ten thousand dollars for it."

"Sahib! What do you mean?"

"Well, I will give you fifteen thousand dollars for it, or if it takes more, I will work for it."

"Sahib," said Rambhau, stiffening his whole body, "this pearl is beyond price. No man in all the world has money enough to pay what this pearl is worth to me. On the market a million dollars could not buy it. I will not sell it to you. You may only have it as a gift."

"No, Rambhau, I cannot accept that. As much as I want the pearl, I cannot accept it that way. Perhaps I am proud, but that is too easy. I must pay for it, or work for it…."

The old pearl-diver was stunned. "You don't understand at all, Sahib. Don't you see? My only son gave his life to get this pearl, and I wouldn't sell it for any money. Its worth is in the lifeblood of my son. I cannot sell this—but I can give it to you. Just accept it in token of the love I bear you."

The missionary was choked, and for a moment could not speak. Then he gripped the hand of the old man. "Rambhau," he said in a low voice, "don't you see? My words are just what you have been saying to

God all the time."

The diver looked long and searchingly at the missionary, and slowly, slowly he began to understand. "God is offering to you salvation as a free gift," said the missionary. "It is so great and priceless that no man on earth can buy it. Millions of dollars are too little. No man on earth could earn it. His life would be millions of years too short. No man is good enough to deserve it. It cost God the lifeblood of His only Son to make the entrance for you into heaven. In a million years, in a hundred pilgrimages, you could not earn that entrance. All you can do is to accept it as a token of God's love for you—a sinner.

"Rambhau, of course I will accept the pearl in deep humility, praying God I may be worthy of your love. Rambhau, won't you accept God's great gift of heaven, too, in deep humility, knowing it cost Him the death of His Son to offer it to you?"

Great tears were now rolling down the cheeks of the old man. The veil was beginning to lift. "Sahib, I see it now. I have believed in the doctrine of Jesus for the last two years, but I could not believe that His salvation was free. Now I understand. Some things are too priceless to be bought or earned. Sahib, I will accept His salvation!"

WHO AM I?

AUTHOR UNKNOWN

Who am I? I was born in 1725, and I died 1807. The only godly influence in my life, as far back as I can remember, was my mother, whom I had for only seven years. When she left my life through death, I was virtually an orphan. My father remarried, sent me to a strict military school, where the severity of discipline almost broke my back. I couldn't stand it any longer, and I left in rebellion at the age of ten. One year later, deciding that I would never enter formal education again, I became a seaman apprentice, hoping somehow to step into my father's trade and learn at least the ability to skillfully navigate a ship.

By and by, through a process of time, I slowly gave myself over to the devil. And I determined that I would sin to my fill without restraint, now that the righteous lamp of my life had gone out. I did that until my days in the military service, where again discipline worked hard against me, but I further rebelled. My spirit would not break, and I became increasingly more and more a rebel. Because of a number of things that I disagreed with in the military, I finally deserted, only to be captured like a common criminal and beaten publicly several times.

After enduring the punishment, I again fled. I entertained thoughts of suicide on my way to Africa, deciding that would be the place I could get farthest from anyone that knew me. And again I made a pact with the devil to live for him.

Somehow, through a process of events, I got in touch with a Portuguese slave trader, and I lived in his home. He was married to a black wife, who was brimming with hostility and took a lot of it out on me. She beat me, and I ate like a dog on the floor of the home. If I refused to do that, she would whip me with a lash.

I fled penniless, owning only the clothes on my back, to the shoreline of Africa where I built a fire, hoping to attract a ship that was passing by. The skipper thought that I had gold or slaves or ivory to sell and was surprised because I was a skilled navigator. And it was there that I virtually lived for a long period of time. It was a slave ship. It was not uncommon for as many as six hundred blacks from Africa to be in the hold of the ship, down below, being taken to America.

I went through all sorts of narrow escapes with death only a hairbreadth away on a number of occasions. One time I opened some crates of rum and got everybody on the crew drunk. The skipper, incensed with my actions, beat me, threw me down below, and I lived on stale bread and sour vegetables for an unendurable amount of time. He brought me above to beat me again, and I fell overboard. Because I couldn't swim, he harpooned me to get me back on the ship. And I lived with the scar in my side, big enough for me to put my fist into, until the day of my death.

On board, I was inflamed with fever. I was enraged with the humiliation. A storm broke out, and I wound up again in the hold of the ship, down among the pumps. To keep the ship afloat, I worked along as a servant of the slaves. There, bruised and confused, bleeding, diseased, I was the epitome of the degenerate man. I remembered the words of my mother. I cried out to God, the only way I knew, calling upon His grace and His mercy to deliver me, and upon His son to save me. The only glimmer of light I could find was in a crack in the ship in the floor above me, and I looked up to it and screamed for help. God heard me.

Thirty-one years passed, I married a childhood sweetheart. I entered the ministry. In every place that I served, rooms had to be added to the building to handle the crowds that came to hear the gospel that was presented and the story of God's grace in my life.

My tombstone above my head reads, "Born 1725, died 1807. A clerk, once an infidel and libertine, a servant of slaves in Africa, was by the rich mercy of our Lord and Savior, Jesus Christ, preserved, restored, pardoned, and appointed to preach the faith he once long labored to destroy."

I decided before my death to put my life's story in verse. And that verse has become a hymn.

My name? John Newton.

The hymn? "Amazing Grace."

Amazing grace! how sweet the sound—
That saved a wretch like me!
I once was lost, but now am found;
Was blind, but now I see.
'Twas grace that taught my heart to fear,
And grace my fears relieved;
How precious did that grace appear
The hour I first believed.
Through many dangers, toils and snares,
I have already come;
'Tis grace has brought me safe thus far,
And grace will lead me home.
When we've been there ten thousand years,
Bright shining as the sun,
We've no less days to sing God's praise
Than when we'd first begun.

—JOHN NEWTON

RUBY'S REMARKABLE GRACE

JANE CONNER
FROM *MOODY* MAGAZINE

Ruby was a fifty-seven-year-old widow. I came on the scene in 1978—the girlfriend of Ruby's twenty-seven-year-old son. No two women could have been less alike, and yet she passed on a legacy to me.

A devout Christian, she attended church every time the doors were open. I was a hard-drinking, foul-mouthed, twenty-year-old who was living with Ruby's son, Jim, without being married. I don't know how she even looked at me. I can only imagine how many hours she spent on her knees praying for Jim and me.

At first, I was amused by her. She would flinch a bit when I used profanity, and she tried to insert a Bible verse or two in our conversations. As the months progressed and our relationship deepened, she began inviting me to church.

I usually made excuses to avoid going, but finally, because I loved her son and hoped to earn brownie points with the woman who could be my future mother-in-law, I agreed to attend a special service featuring a missionary speaker.

I had never attended such a church, or heard a message like the one the missionary gave. He said Jesus died on the cross for *me*. He emphasized God's unselfish love in giving his Son to die for *my* sins. Feeling unworthy of God's love, I almost cried, but that would have ruined my tough lady image. I couldn't break down in front of Ruby.

So, I held back my tears and nonchalantly shrugged when she asked me if I enjoyed the service.

Before I got to the door, however, I saw God's love in action. People I didn't know welcomed me and showed an interest in me. I was overwhelmed by the friendliness of Ruby's church family. I attended church as a child, but my family merely "put in time." We arrived as late as we could and left immediately without speaking to anyone.

At home, I thought about the missionary's words. I couldn't imagine God loving me enough to send his Son to die for me. And I thought about the church members. They welcomed me even though I didn't dress or speak the way they did. Both the message and the people made me hope for a type of love I hungered for.

Ruby continued to welcome me into her home, even on the mornings when Jim would stop to pick up his younger brother for work and it was obvious that he and I were hung over from a night of partying. Her acceptance of me, in spite of her disapproval of my lifestyle, amazed me. Ruby's love and her church's kindness encouraged me to seek a closer walk with God.

In the spring, Ruby told us her church would be helping to start an outreach church. She encouraged us to attend. We visited this new church on Easter—their first Sunday service. As the pastor preached on God's love and forgiveness, I sat through the service thinking, "I'm not worthy! God shouldn't have sent anyone to die for me. I'm not good enough for that gift!"

Inside I was weeping, but I didn't cry on the outside until after the service.

When the pastor, Bob Ivers, shook my hand at the back of the church, he politely said, "Thanks for coming! How are you today?"

I immediately broke into tears and said, "Not very good!"

"Do you want to talk about it?" he said.

"I'm not good enough for God to love!" I said through my tears.

We sat down, and opening his Bible, the pastor showed me that none of us are "good enough" for God to love. God's love is a free gift that we don't deserve and can't earn. The pastor read John 3:16–17, which described God's gift of eternal life and reminded me Jesus came to save, not condemn the world. In 1 John 1:9, he explained God's promise to forgive our sins if we confess them and turn from them. Tenderly, Pastor Ivers led me in prayer to ask Jesus to be my Lord and Savior. God forgave me, and I held to his promise of eternal life.

I felt peace and deep joy and couldn't wait to tell Jim. He was cautiously pleased. As a preacher's son, he knew the difference God would make in my life, bringing peace and joy, but he wondered how it might change our relationship.

When I told Ruby the news, her hug and the tears running down her face spoke volumes.

Over the next few weeks, the best gifts Ruby gave me were time and prayer. She didn't expect immediate perfection. She didn't demand that I leave Jim, give up drinking, pray and read my Bible every day, and attend every church service. She continued to pray for me, love me, and accept me as a baby Christian who had a long way to grow.

But I knew I needed to make some changes. Within two months I moved out of Jim's place. Angry, he accused me of acting holier-than-thou. He wasn't happy about my getting baptized, reading the Bible, and going to church. He wasn't ready for the rapid changes.

I quit drinking, but he drank more. Whenever I called in the evenings, he wasn't home, and I knew he was at the bars. It was a dark and lonely time for me. I had Jesus, but I didn't have the man I loved.

It hurt a lot. But I decided that as God's child, I had made the right decision. My old life had to die and with it my old relationship, too. I prayed God would give Jim back to me, but for now I had to surrender him.

After moving out, I lived alone in a tent in a campground because I couldn't afford to pay rent. I didn't want to live with Ruby or others whom Jim might blame for my desertion of him. It was a difficult time, and yet Jesus walked with me through that lonely valley.

Two months later, Jim asked me if we could date again. We knelt together and asked Jesus to be the head of our lives and to help us remain sexually pure until we were married. Four months later, Pastor Ivers married us in a joyful ceremony.

Today, Ruby is my mother-in-law, or should I say, my mother-in-love. Nineteen years later, I'm thankful she is still loving us and praying for us through good times and bad.

Our son is a teenager and sometimes I worry about his future relationships. I see young adults who are unkempt and foul mouthed, and my first instinct is to avoid them, feeling very self-righteous. And then God gently reminds me that I was just like them, and someone loved me anyway. Someone welcomed me into her home even when I was unlovable.

It's my turn to show that kind of love. It isn't easy, so I'm spending lots of time in prayer. With God's help, I'll pass on Ruby's legacy of unconditional love.

Forgiveness

GOD'S TENDERNESS

God pardons like a mother,
who kisses the offense into everlasting forgiveness.

—Henry Ward Beecher

THE GOLD WATCH

SUSAN WALES
FROM *A MATCH MADE IN HEAVEN*

When my husband, Henry, retired from his job as a mechanic, the owners of the Ford dealership where he had worked gave him a gold watch inscribed with his name. Henry was so proud of that shiny gold watch that it became his greatest treasure. "Now I have something special to leave my son," he beamed.

But the gift our son wanted was for us to relocate. Violence had been on the rise in the Los Angeles community where my husband and I had raised our family, and now our grown children urged us to enjoy our retirement years in a beautiful, safe place. But Henry refused. He said the right thing to do was to stay put and try to make a positive difference.

One small way to do this was with our roses. Every day, Henry and I worked in the rose garden in front of our house. Soon it was one of the few bright spots on our street. If someone in the neighborhood had a birthday, a graduation, a birth, or a death in the family, Henry would deliver a bouquet of our roses to the family. Before long, Henry and I became known as the "Rose Couple."

One night around 10 P.M. a friend called, asking Henry for help. "Charlie's broken down at the corner of Thirtieth and Crenshaw," Henry explained, heading for the door. "It sounds like the carburetor. Shouldn't take me too long."

"How about picking up some milk on the way home?" I asked.

"Sure," Henry said, "but don't wait up, honey"

When I hadn't heard from Henry by 11:30, I began to worry. Henry always called if he was delayed. I began to pace the floor and pray while I waited. After an eternity there was a knock on the door.

"Lucille," a familiar voice called out. Through my peephole, I saw our pastor.

I can scarcely recall the rest of that evening. My worst fears were confirmed. During an apparent robbery attempt, Henry and Charlie had been gunned down by neighborhood gang members. Both were dead.

Our son, Ed, went to the morgue to identify his father and collect his things. When he arrived home, Ed informed me that the killers had not only taken Henry's wallet but the gold retirement watch.

In the weeks following Henry's death, my grief was indescribable. Ed also grieved deeply for his father. He tried to reassure me that the loss of the gold watch didn't matter. "Daddy gave me so much good stuff that I keep tucked away in here," he said, pointing to his heart. "I don't need the watch, Mama."

But for some reason, I did. I couldn't be comforted about Henry—or the watch. Often I prayed, "Please, dear Lord, help the police find Henry's killers. And please, I beg you, help me get back my Henry's watch!"

Weeks passed with no arrests. Still I couldn't let go of the idea of recovering the watch. Perhaps it was my way to hang on to hope. Or to Henry. As I walked to church or the market or visited a neighbor, I would instinctively check the wrist of everyone who passed by. I even browsed through the local pawn shops.

Eventually my children decided to offer a $250 reward for the return of the gold watch. Six months passed, and no one responded. The owners of the Ford dealership presented me with another gold watch just like the first one. Although I was touched with their kindness and generosity, it wasn't the same as finding the watch Henry had owned and worn so proudly.

Meanwhile, my roses had fallen into gross neglect. It was too painful for me to garden without my Henry.

One weekend, Sharon, our oldest daughter, came to stay with me. She suggested we get up early on Saturday to prune. "Mama, you've got to live again," she told me as we trimmed the roses and pulled weeds.

As we worked that morning, I noticed a young African-American man walk past our garden two or three times. He paused as if he wanted to say something.

Finally I spoke to him. "Son, would you like some of my roses?"

"Are you the Rose Lady?" he asked.

I nodded and replied, "I am. And who might you be?"

"Name's Jared," he mumbled. He hesitated a moment before he reached out and took the bouquet I was holding out to him. Then he left without a word.

The next Saturday afternoon the young man appeared again. "You sure like my roses, son," I laughed as he stood staring. He appeared so nervous and jumpy that I suddenly became afraid.

"Rose Lady" he finally said, "I need to talk to you. It's important."

We sat in silence on my porch for a few minutes. Suddenly he reached in his pocket and pulled out a handkerchief. He cleared his throat and said, "Got something here that belongs to you."

In the folds of the handkerchief was Henry's watch. Tears streamed down my face as I lifted the precious gold timepiece and held it close to my heart.

"I didn't kill him," he declared. "I swear. You believe me, don't you?"

"Well, I don't suppose you did. No killer would bring this watch to me," I said.

Then Jared told his story. He was with his gang when they decided to rob Henry and Charlie. But Jared was shocked and angry when one of the gang members pulled a gun and killed the two men. "They told me to go over and get their wallets and check for jewelry," he explained, "but when I was unfastening the watch, your husband…he said something, ma'am. He whispered, 'Get my watch to the Rose Lady. Tell her I love her.'"

The young man was trembling, and tears filled his eyes. "I hid the watch from them," he continued. "I was going to bring it to you sooner, but I was afraid. Are you going to turn me in to the police?"

I thought for a moment about what Henry would do and then spoke. "I'm going to ask you to do the right thing."

"It's not that easy, you know. If I go to the police, those boys will relocate me to the cemetery," he responded.

"I'm sure it's not easy" I agreed, "but I've always found that when you do the right thing, God will take care of the rest."

I never saw that young man again. He did go to the police, and his friends were eventually arrested for the murders, but Jared was not charged. It seemed to me at the time that just as he had given me back Henry's watch, God had given Jared back his life.

Sometime later I ran into one of Jared's relatives. "Where is the young man these days?" I asked.

"Oh, he's in college now!" she said proudly.

"You tell him the Rose Lady said hello," I told her.

After I got Henry's watch back, I finally began to heal. Years later I heard the good news that young Jared had graduated from college. Suddenly I had an idea. I found the duplicate gold watch the Ford dealer had given me, boxed it up, and sent it to the new graduate with best wishes from the Rose Lady.

My roses and my heart were in bloom again.

Be kind and compassionate to one another,
forgiving each other, just as in Christ God forgave you.

EPHESIANS 4:32

PICTURE OF LOVE

EDWARD C. MCMANUS
FROM *THE JOKESMITH*

woman is dying of AIDS. A priest is summoned. He attempts to comfort her, but to no avail.

"I am lost," she said. "I have ruined my life and every life around me. Now I'm going painfully to hell. There is no hope for me."

The priest saw a framed picture of a pretty girl on the dresser. "Who is this?" he asked. The woman brightened. "She's my daughter, the one beautiful thing in my life."

"And would you help her if she was in trouble, or made a mistake? Would you forgive her? Would you still love her?"

"Of course I would!" cried the woman. "I would do anything for her! Why do you ask such a question?"

"Because I wanted you to know," said the priest, "that God has a picture of you on His dresser."

MENDING FENCES

BILLY GRAHAM
FROM *THE SECRETS OF HAPPINESS*

know of two deacons who had quarreled over an old line fence; they had not spoken to each other for a long time. One of them, wanting to make peace, took his Bible and went to visit his neighbor. Handing his Bible to his "old enemy," he said, "John, you read and I'll pray. We must be friends."

But John, fumbling for his glasses, said, "But I can't read. I haven't my spectacles."

"Take mine," said his peace-loving neighbor.

After they had read the Word and prayed together, they arose and embraced each other. John handed back the spectacles to his neighbor and said through his tears, "Jim, that old line fence looks different through your glasses."

When we have the peace of God, we can see things through "the other man's glasses," and by doing that we can make peace.

Regret

He who cannot forgive another
breaks the bridge over which he must pass himself.

—GEORGE HERBERT

LESSON IN FORGIVENESS

JERRY HARPT

orty-five years seems like a long time to remember the name of a mere acquaintance. I have duly forgotten the name of an old lady who was a customer on my paper route when I was a twelve-year-old boy in Marinette, Wisconsin, back in 1954. Yet it seems like just yesterday that she taught me a lesson in forgiveness that I can only hope to pass on to someone else someday.

On a mindless Saturday afternoon, a friend and I were throwing rocks onto the roof of the old lady's house from a secluded spot in her backyard. The object of our play was to observe how the rocks changed to missiles as they rolled to the roof's edge and shot out into the yard like comets falling from the sky.

I found myself a perfectly smooth rock and sent it for a ride. The stone was too smooth, however, so it slipped from my hand as I let it go and headed straight for a small window on the old lady's back porch. At the sound of fractured glass, we took off from the old lady's yard faster than any of our missiles flew off her roof.

I was too scared about getting caught that first night to be concerned about the old lady with the broken porch window. However, a few days later, when I was sure that I hadn't been discovered, I started to feel guilty for her misfortune. She still greeted me with a smile each day when I gave her the paper, but I was no longer able to act comfortable in her presence.

I made up my mind that I would save my paper delivery money, and in three weeks I had the seven dollars that I calculated would cover the cost of her window. I put the money in an envelope with a note explaining that I was sorry for breaking her window and hoped that the seven dollars would cover the cost for repairing it.

I waited until it was dark, snuck up to the old lady's house, and put the envelope of retribution through the letter slot in her door. My soul felt redeemed, and I couldn't wait for the freedom of, once again, looking straight into the old lady's eyes.

The next day, I handed the old lady her paper and was able to return the warm smile that I was receiving from her. She thanked me for the paper and said, "Here, I have something for you." It was a bag of cookies. I thanked her and proceeded to eat the cookies as I continued my route.

After several cookies, I felt an envelope and pulled it out of the bag. When I opened the envelope, I was stunned. Inside was the seven dollars and a short note that said, "I'm proud of you."

Fragrance

Forgiveness is like the violet
Sending forth its pure fragrance
On the heel of the boot
Of the one who crushed it.

—Author Unknown

SEED OF LOVE

NANETTE THORSEN-SNIPES
FROM *HEART-STIRRING STORIES OF ROMANCE*

My day began on a decidedly sour note when I saw my six-year-old wrestling with a branch of my azalea bush. By the time I got outside, he'd broken it.

"Can I take this to school today?" he asked.

With a wave of my hand, I sent him on. I turned my back so he wouldn't see the tears gathering in my eyes. I loved that azalea bush. I touched the broken limb to silently say, *I'm sorry.*

I wished I could have said that to my husband when he left earlier, but I'd been angry. The washing machine had leaked on my brand-new linoleum. *Why hadn't he just taken the time to fix it the night before instead of playing checkers with Jonathan?* I wondered.

I was still mopping up the mess on the floor when Jonathan followed me into the kitchen. "What's for breakfast, Mom?"

I opened the refrigerator. "Not cereal," I said, watching the sides of his mouth drop. "How about toast and jelly?" I smeared the toast with jelly and set it in front of him. *Why was I so angry?* I tossed my husband's dishes into the sudsy water.

It was days like this that made me want to quit. I just wanted to drive my car up to the mountains, hide myself in a crevice, and never come down.

Somehow I managed to lug the wet clothes to the laundromat. I spent most of the day washing and drying clothes and thinking how love had disappeared from my life. Staring at the graffiti on the walls, I felt as wrung-out as the clothes left in the washers.

As I finished hanging up the last of my husband's shirts, I looked at the clock on the wall. 2:30. I was late. Jonathan's class let out at 2:15. I dumped my clothes in the backseat and hurriedly drove to the school.

I was out of breath by the time I knocked on the teacher's door. I peered in through the glass. With one finger, she motioned for me to wait. She said something to Jonathan and handed him and two other children crayons and a sheet of paper.

What now? I thought as she rustled through the door and took me aside. "I want to talk to you about Jonathan," she said.

I prepared myself for the worst. Nothing would have surprised me. I'd had a fight with my husband and we weren't speaking, my son had broken a limb off my favorite tree, and now this.

"Did you know Jonathan brought flowers to school today?" she asked.

I nodded, trying to keep the hurt in my eyes from showing. I glanced at my son busily coloring a picture. His wavy hair was too long and flopped just beneath his brow. He pushed it away with the back of his hand. His eyes burst with blue as he admired his handiwork.

"Let me tell you about yesterday," the teacher insisted. "See that little girl?"

I watched the rosy-cheeked child laugh and point to a colorful picture taped to the wall. I nodded.

"Well, yesterday she was almost hysterical. Her mother and father are going through a nasty divorce. Tish said she didn't want to live; she wished she could die. I watched that child bury her face in her hands and say loud enough for the class to hear, 'Nobody loves me.' I did all I could to console her, but it only seemed to make things worse."

"I thought you wanted to talk to me about Jonathan," I said.

"I do," she said, touching the sleeve of my blouse. "This morning your son came straight to Tish. I watched him hand her the flowers and whisper, 'I love you, Tish.'"

I felt my heart swell with pride for what my son had done. I smiled at the teacher. "Thank you," I said, reaching for Jonathan's hand. "You've made my day."

Later that evening, I began pulling weeds from around my lopsided azalea bush. As I let my mind wander back to the love Jonathan showed the little girl, I was reminded of a verse from the Bible: "And now these three remain: faith, hope and love. But the greatest of these is love" (1 Corinthians 13:13). My son knew how to show love, but all day I had only showed anger. I dropped my head and whispered, "Forgive me, Lord."

I heard the familiar squeak of my husband's truck brakes as he pulled into the drive. I snapped a small limb bristling with hot pink azaleas off the bush. I felt the seed of love begin to bloom again in me.

My husband's eyes widened in surprise as I handed him the flowers. "I love you," I whispered.

Live in harmony with one another; be sympathetic, love as brothers, be compassionate and humble. Do not repay evil with evil or insult with insult, but with blessing, because to this you were called so that you may inherit a blessing.

1 PETER 3:8–9

FORGETTING

LUIS PALAU

FROM *EXPERIENCING GOD'S FORGIVENESS*

lara Barton, the founder of the American Red cross, was reminded one day of a vicious deed that someone had done to her years before. But she acted as if she had never heard of the incident.

"Don't you remember it?" her friend asked.

"No," came Barton's reply. "I distinctly remember forgetting it."

THE WAITING FATHER

PHILIP YANCEY
FROM *WHAT'S SO AMAZING ABOUT GRACE?*

*N*ot long ago I heard from a pastor friend who was battling with his fifteen-year-old daughter. He knew she was using birth control, and several nights she had not bothered to come home at all. The parents had tried various forms of punishment, to no avail. The daughter lied to them, deceived them, and found a way to turn the tables on them: "It's your fault for being so strict!"

My friend told me, "I remember standing before the plate-glass window in my living room, staring out into the darkness, waiting for her to come home. I felt such rage. I wanted to be like the father of the Prodigal Son, yet I was furious with my daughter for the way she would manipulate us and twist the knife to hurt us. And of course, she was hurting herself more than anyone. I understood then the passages in the prophets expressing God's anger. The people knew how to wound him, and God cried out in pain.

"And yet I must tell you, when my daughter came home that night, or rather the next morning, I wanted nothing in the world so much as to take her in my arms, to love her, to tell her I wanted the best for her. I was a helpless, lovesick father."

Now, when I think about God, I hold up that image of the lovesick father which is miles away from the stern monarch I used to envision. I think of my friend standing in front of the plate-glass window gazing achingly into the darkness. I think of Jesus' depiction of the Waiting Father, heartsick, abused, yet wanting above all else to forgive and begin anew, to announce with joy, "This is my son who was dead, and is alive again; he was lost, and is found."

Mozart's *Requiem* contains a wonderful line that has become my prayer, one I pray with increasing confidence: "Remember, merciful Jesu, that I am the cause of your journey." I think he remembers.

Merciful

The LORD is compassionate and gracious,
slow to anger, abounding in love.
He will not always accuse,
nor will he harbor his anger forever;
he does not treat us as our sins deserve
or repay us according to our iniquities.
For as high as the heavens are above the earth,
so great is his love for those who fear him;
as far as the east is from the west,
so far has he removed our transgressions from us.

PSALM 103:8–12

OUT OF THE CARPENTRY SHOP

MAX LUCADO
FROM *GOD CAME NEAR*

The heavy door creaked on its hinges as he pushed it open. With a few strides he crossed the silent shop and opened the wooden shutters to a square shaft of sunshine that pierced the darkness, painting a box of daylight on the dirt floor.

He looked around the carpentry shop. He stood a moment in the refuge of the little room that housed so many sweet memories. He balanced the hammer in his hand. He ran his fingers across the sharp teeth of the saw. He stroked the smoothly worn wood of the sawhorse. He had come to say goodbye.

It was time for him to leave. He had heard something that made him know it was time to go. So he came one last time to smell the sawdust and lumber.

Life was peaceful here. Life was so…safe.

Here he had spent countless hours of contentment. On this dirt floor he had played as a toddler while his father worked. Here Joseph had taught him how to grip a hammer. And on this workbench he had built his first chair.

I wonder what he thought as he took one last look around the room. Perhaps he stood for a moment at the workbench looking at the tiny shadows cast by the chisel and shavings. Perhaps he listened as voices from the past filled the air.

"Good job, Jesus."

"Joseph, Jesus—come and eat!"

"Don't worry, sir, we'll get it finished on time. I'll get Jesus to help me."

I wonder if he hesitated. I wonder if his heart was torn. I wonder if he rolled a nail between his thumb and fingers, anticipating the pain.

It was in the carpentry shop that he must have given birth to his thoughts. Here concepts and convictions were woven together to form the fabric of his ministry.

You can almost see the tools of the trade in his words as he spoke. You can see the trueness of a plumb line as he called for moral standards. You can hear the whistle of the plane as he pleads for religion to shave away unnecessary traditions. You can picture the snugness of a dovetail as he demands loyalty in relationships. You can imagine him with a pencil and a ledger as he urges honesty.

It was here that his human hands shaped the wood his divine hands had created. And it was here that his body matured while his spirit waited for the right moment, the right day.

And now that day had arrived.

It must have been difficult to leave. After all, life as a carpenter wasn't bad. It wasn't bad at all. Business was good. The future was bright and his work was enjoyable.

In Nazareth he was known only as Jesus, the son of Joseph. You can be sure he was respected in the community. He was good with his hands. He had many friends. He was a favorite among the children. He could tell a good joke and had a habit of filling the air with contagious laughter.

I wonder if he wanted to stay. "I could do a good job here in Nazareth. Settle down. Raise a family. Be a civic leader."

I wonder because I know he had already read the last chapter. He knew that the feet that would step out of the safe shadow of the carpentry shop would not rest until they'd been pierced and placed on a Roman cross.

You see, he didn't have to go. He had a choice. He could have stayed. He could have kept his mouth shut. He could have ignored the call or at least postponed it. And had he chosen to stay, who would've known? Who would have blamed him?

He could have come back as a man in another era when society wasn't so volatile, when religion wasn't so stale, when people would listen better.

He could have come back when crosses were out of style.

But his heart wouldn't let him. If there was hesitation on the part of his humanity, it was overcome by the compassion of his divinity. His divinity heard the voices. His divinity heard the hopeless cries of the poor, the bitter accusations of the abandoned, the dangling despair of those who are trying to save themselves.

And his divinity saw the faces. Some wrinkled. Some weeping. Some hidden behind veils. Some obscured by fear. Some earnest with searching. Some blank with boredom. From the face of Adam to the face of the infant born somewhere in the world as you read these words, he saw them all.

And you can be sure of one thing. Among the voices that found their way into that carpentry shop in Nazareth was your voice. Your silent prayers uttered on tearstained pillows were heard before they were said. Your deepest questions about death and eternity were answered before they were asked. And your direst need, your need for a Savior, was met before you ever sinned.

And not only did he hear you, he saw you. He saw your face aglow the hour you first knew him. He saw your face in the shame the hour you first fell. The same face that looked back at you from this morning's mirror, looked at him. And it was enough to kill him.

He left because of you.

He laid his security down with his hammer. He hung tranquility on the peg with his apron. He closed the window shutters on the sunshine of his youth and locked the door on the comfort and ease of anonymity.

Since he could bear your sins more easily than he could bear the thought of your hopelessness, he chose to leave.

It wasn't easy. Leaving the carpentry shop never has been.

Trust and Contentment

A NEW DAY

Every morning lean your arms awhile
Upon the window sill of heaven
And gaze upon the Lord.
Then, with the vision in your heart
Turn strong to meet your day.

—Author Unknown

KEVIN'S DIFFERENT WORLD

KELLY ADKINS
FROM *CAMPUS LIFE*

y brother Kevin thinks God lives under his bed.
At least that's what I heard him say one night.
He was praying out loud in his dark bedroom, and I stopped outside his
closed door to listen.

"Are you there, God?" he said. "Where are you? Oh, I see. Under the
bed."

I giggled softly and tiptoed off to my own room. Kevin's unique per-
spectives are often a source of amusement. But that night something else
lingered long after the humor. I realized for the first time the very different world Kevin lives in.

He was born thirty years ago, mentally disabled as a result of diffi-
culties during labor. Apart from his size (he's six-foot-two), there are few
ways in which he is an adult. He reasons and communicates with the
capabilities of a seven-year-old, and he always will.

He will probably always believe that God lives under his bed, that
Santa Claus is the one who fills the space under our tree every Christmas,
and that airplanes stay up in the sky because angels carry them.

I remember wondering if Kevin realizes he is different. Is he ever dissatisfied with his monotonous life? Up before dawn each day, off to work at a workshop for the disabled, home to walk our cocker spaniel, returning to eat his favorite macaroni and cheese for dinner, and later to bed. The only variation in the entire scheme are laundry days, when he hovers excitedly over the washing machine like a mother with her newborn child.

He does not seem dissatisfied. He lopes out to the bus every morning at 7:05, eager for a day of simple work. He wrings his hands excitedly while the water boils on the stove for dinner, and he stays up late twice a week to gather our dirty laundry for his next day's laundry chores.

And Saturdays—oh, the bliss of Saturdays! That's the day my dad takes Kevin to the airport to have a soft drink, watch the planes land, and speculate loudly on the destination of each passenger inside.

"That one's goin' to Chi-car-go!" Kevin shouts as he claps his hands. His anticipation is so great he can hardly sleep on Friday nights.

I don't think Kevin knows anything exists outside his world of daily rituals and weekend field trips. He doesn't know what it means to be discontent. His life is simple. He will never know the entanglement of wealth or power, and he does not care what brand of clothing he wears or what kind of food he eats. He recognizes no differences in people, treating each person as an equal and a friend. His needs have always been met, and he never worries that one day they may not be.

His hands are diligent. Kevin is never so happy as when he is working. When he unloads the dishwasher or vacuums the carpet, his heart is completely in it. He does not shrink from a job when it is begun, and he does not leave a job until it is finished. But when his tasks are done, Kevin knows how to relax. He is not obsessed with his work or the work of others.

His heart is pure. He still believes everyone tells the truth, promises must be kept, and when you are wrong, you apologize instead of argue. Free from pride and unconcerned with appearances, Kevin is not afraid to cry when he is hurt, angry, or sorry. He is always transparent, always sincere.

And he trusts God. Not confined by intellectual reasoning, when he comes to Christ, he comes as a child.

Kevin seems to know God—to really be friends with him—in a way that is difficult for an "educated" person to grasp. God seems like his closest companion.

In my moments of doubt and frustrations with my Christianity, I envy the security Kevin has in his simple faith. It is then that I am most willing to admit that he has some divine knowledge that rises above my mortal questions. It is then I realize that perhaps he is not the one with the handicap—I am.

One day, when the mysteries of heaven are opened, and we are all amazed at how close God really is to our hears, I'll realize that God heard the simple prayers of a boy who believed that God lived under his bed.

Kevin won't be surprised at all.

A BRIEF BLESSING

GIGI GRAHAM TCHIVIDJIAN
FROM *CURRENTS OF THE HEART*

Fear not, for I am with you;
Be not dismayed, for I am your God.
I will strengthen you,
Yes, I will help you,
I will uphold you with My righteous right hand.
ISAIAH 41:10, NKJV

When I was going through a difficult time, I remembered this brief blessing an older pastor friend had shared with me. In just one verse of just one book of the Bible, we can receive so much help, strength, and encouragement.

In this one verse we have the promise of:

His presence...*I am with you.*

His power...*I will strengthen you.*

His protection...*I will uphold you and help you.*

And these promises are also very personal. Notice the *you*. "So," this pastor told me, "we can choose to be problem-conscious or power-conscious."

Which are you?

YESTERDAY AND TOMORROW

ROBERT J. BURDETTE

There are two days in every week about which we should not worry—two days that should be kept free from any fear and apprehension. One of these days is Yesterday, with its mistakes and cares, its aches and pains, its faults and blunders. Yesterday has passed forever beyond our control. All the money in the world cannot bring back Yesterday. We cannot undo a single act we performed; we cannot erase a single word we said; we cannot rectify a single mistake. Yesterday has passed forever beyond recall. Let it go.

The other day we should not worry about is Tomorrow, with its possible adversities, its burdens, its large promise, and poor performance. Tomorrow also is beyond our immediate control. Tomorrow's sun will rise either in splendor or behind a mass of clouds—but it will rise. And until it does, we have no stake in Tomorrow, because it is as yet unborn.

That leaves us but one day—Today! And a person can fight the battles of just one day.

Yesterday and Tomorrow are futile worries. Let us, therefore, resolve to journey no more than one day at a time.

Therefore do not worry about tomorrow, for tomorrow will worry about itself. Each day has enough trouble of its own.
MATTHEW 6:34

CONTRASTS

JONI EARECKSON TADA
FROM *GLORIOUS INTRUDER*

n artist paints so that people might *see*. You share beauty, elevate the imagination, inspire and challenge the senses— and seek to do it all without being blatant or obvious. The good artist will let the viewer discover truth for himself.

I think of a recent painting of a horse. As I painted, there were parts on that horse I thought especially attractive— parts I wanted the viewer to notice. Like that nice place where neck turns into chest. And those slender ankles. The tilt of the head was another point of interest.

As an artist I thought to myself, *how can I get the viewer to look at these places without being obvious?*

I noticed the horse's coat was a warm, golden color. What's the opposite color of gold? Violet, of course— cool, dark contrast to the horse's coat.

That's what I'll do, I reasoned. *I'll lay this cool violet next to the special places on the horse. That will draw attention without being too conspicuous.*

As I worked on the horse's neck, I brushed a hint of violet alongside the gold. When placed alongside each other, these colors, subtle and mysterious, would attract your attention. Artistically, it was a successful attempt to have the viewer see what I wanted him to see.

God, too, is a Master Artist. And there are aspects of your life and character— good, quality things— he wants others to notice. So without using blatant tricks or obvious gimmicks, God brings the cool, dark contrast of suffering into your life. That contrast, laid up against the golden character of Christ within you, will draw attention...to Him.

Light against darkness. Beauty against affliction. Joy against sorrow. A sweet, patient spirit against pain and disappointment—major contrasts that have a way of attracting notice.

Your life begins to snap with interest. People notice you out of the corner of their eye— are drawn to you— without really understanding why.

They are, in fact, seeing what the Master Artist wants them to observe: Christ in you, highlighted against an opposing force of dark suffering.

You are the canvas on which He paints glorious truths, sharing beauty, and inspiring others.

So that people might see Him.

Consecrated

Take my life and let it be
Consecrated, Lord, to Thee;
Take my moments and my days—
Let them flow in ceaseless praise.
Take my love—Lord, I pour
At Thy feet its treasure store;
Take myself—and I will be
Ever, only, all for Thee.

—FRANCES RIDLEY HAVERGAL (1836-1879)

SEVEN WONDERS
OF THE WORLD

AUTHOR UNKNOWN

The teacher asked her students to make a list of the seven natural wonders of the world. The class set to work on the project for quite a while, and as time wore on some of the students finished the list. The teacher said the children could go outside for recess as each one finished. Eventually, only one little girl was still at her desk writing. Then she smiled, wrote something, and jumped up, joyfully announcing that she was done and skipped happily out to play with the others. The teacher picked up the paper and read the following:

1. *Seeing*

2. *Hearing*

3. *Tasting*

4. *Touching*

5. *Running*

6. *Laughing*

7. *Loving*

BLOSSOMS

BARBARA BAUMGARDNER
FROM *BEREAVEMENT MAGAZINE*

I thought it was a Christmas cactus. The tag read, "Zygocactus," and I didn't know what it meant. But it was at Thanksgiving time that first year after my husband died when it bloomed so profusely—huge, gentle, pink blossoms.

I tried to find a smile, remembering how overly-eager I had always been to begin decorating for my favorite holiday. This year, though, my heart was heavy with the prospect of my first Christmas as a widow.

One day, I showed a friend the display of warm, pink blossoms hanging like ornaments on the cactus by the window. She suggested my plant might be a Thanksgiving cactus and then wondered aloud if it might have been touched by the Master Gardener to help bring some color into my presently drab world. That thought comforted me through the holiday season.

Shortly after Christmas, I picked off the spent, dry blossoms. They crumbled in my hand like sun-parched leaves in late fall. I was feeling like those leaves; dry, worn, and unattractive as I often did after the holidays. But added to those feelings this year was a tremendous void—the kind left by a husband who had died.

Watering can in hand, I approached the sunny window one day in late January and gasped. The cactus was again a mass of pink blossoms. "What in the world are you doing?" I questioned loudly.

As I stared in awe at the wondrous pink and green display, I felt a warmth coming through the window onto my hands and arms. In the friendship of that light, I sensed another Presence. The room was filled with the brilliance of that moment. That must be why my cactus was thriving so beautifully. It lived in daily sunshine.

Now, when I think about that day, I am reminded that I, too, can let my life blossom. I just must allow God's Son to be the light of my day.

May our Lord Jesus Christ himself and God our
Father, who loved us and by his grace gave us
eternal encouragement and good hope,
encourage your hearts and strengthen you
in every good deed and word.

2 THESSALONIANS 2:16–17

SPRINGTIME

JOSEPH BAYLY

FROM *THE LAST THING WE TALK ABOUT*

One Saturday morning in January, I saw the mail truck stop at our mailbox up on the road.

Without thinking, except that I wanted to get the mail, I ran out of the house and up to the road in my shirt sleeves. It was bitterly cold—the temperature was below zero—there was a brisk wind from the north, and the ground was covered with more than a foot of snow.

I opened the mailbox, pulled out the mail, and was about to make a mad dash for the house when I saw what was on the bottom, under the letters: a Burpee seed catalog.

On the front were bright zinnias. I turned it over. On the back were huge tomatoes.

For a few moments I was oblivious to the cold, delivered from it. I leafed through the catalog, tasting corn and cucumbers, smelling roses. I saw the freshly plowed earth, smelled it, let it run through my fingers.

For those brief moments, I was living in the springtime and summer, winter past.

Then the cold penetrated to my bones and I ran back to the house.

When the door was closed behind me, and I was getting warm again, I thought how my moments at the mailbox were like our experience as Christians.

We feel the cold, along with those who do not share our hope. The biting wind penetrates us as them....

But in our cold times, we have a seed catalog. We open it and smell the promised spring, eternal spring. And the first fruit that settles our hope is Jesus Christ, who was raised from death and cold earth to glory eternal.

A BLESSING
FROM THE BIRDS

GIGI GRAHAM TCHIVIDJIAN
FROM *CURRENTS OF THE HEART*

Said the robin to the sparrow,

"I should really like to know

Why these anxious human beings

Rush around and worry so."

Said the sparrow to the robin,

"Friend, I think that it must be

That they have no heavenly Father

Such as cares for you and me."

—ELIZABETH CHENEY

fter days of steady rain there were now patches of blue in the overcast sky outside my kitchen window. The sun was even beginning to peek out timidly between the clouds.

The chimes on the grandfather clock reminded me that the children would soon be bounding in from school, tired and hungry. It was almost time to start fixing their dinner, but maybe I could take just a few minutes....

When I slid open the glass door, a surge of warm, humid air greeted me. I was concerned about a number of things and felt the need to take advantage of this quiet moment, knowing it wouldn't last for long.

I sat down in one of the old rocking chairs on the porch. Glancing appreciatively around the yard, I noticed that everything seemed to be celebrating the return of the sun. The grass was a bright and vivid shade of green; the bougainvillea bush was once again loaded with blossoms. Masses of fuchsia, white and orange, intertwined and tumbled down both sides of the fence. *It looks almost gaudy,* I thought as I watched a very brave (or very stupid) gray squirrel sneak up and steal a piece of dog food right from under the nose of Jessie, our good-natured but overweight rottweiler.

Then a bold blue jay swooped down, grabbed what morsel he could from Jessie's bowl, and quickly flew off again before Jessie—or even the squirrel—had time to notice.

A pair of gentle mourning doves tiptoed timidly around the edge of the porch, and on the top of the olive trees, a mockingbird sang its heart out.

A family of very fat black-and-white ducks with red heads loitered off to the left in the shade of a ficus tree, the staging area for their daily excursion across the backyard. One of them, apparently the appointed lookout, slowly edged closer. When he felt it was safe, he signaled the others. Quickly, they queued up into a long line and waddled across the terrace as fast as their webbed feet would go. They too stopped at Jessie's dish, hoping to find leftovers.

I laughed as I watched their obvious disappointment upon discovering an empty bowl (the blue jay and squirrel had beaten them to it that day). They slowly retreated and waited patiently in the grass, sending their scout from time to time to see if Jessie's dish had been replenished.

While sitting there, rocking gently back and forth, contemplating my concerns and observing this mixture of wildlife scurrying and flitting around the yard, I remembered the passage in Matthew 6 that tells us not to worry.

How I needed to be reminded of that—especially at that moment! I find myself becoming overly concerned, anxious about unpaid bills...my parents' health...a wayward child...my husband's job situation...the lump discovered in my friend's breast...the children's safety...my writing deadlines...my elderly mother-in-law's pending surgery...all of my various responsibilities and my own lack of physical and emotional strength.

My thoughts were suddenly distracted by the loud, rhythmic tapping of a ladder-backed woodpecker working his way up the side of a palm tree while a regal, great blue heron walked stealthily along the edge of the lake. Then a flash of bright orange caught my attention. On the fence, contrasted against the brilliant pink backdrop of the bougainvillea blossoms, two orioles waited to attack the berries on a neighboring bush.

I thought again of the passage in Matthew: "Look at the birds! They don't worry about what to eat—they don't need to sow or reap or store up food—for your heavenly Father feeds them. And you are far more valuable to him than they are. Will all your worries add a single moment to your life?" (Matthew 6:26–27, *The Living Bible*).

Not long ago, while preaching from this passage, our pastor asked if we ever wondered why the Lord had chosen birds in this particular lesson. Personally, I had never thought about it. But Pastor Mike suggested that maybe it was because birds, who are small creatures, limited in size and strength, are capable of doing only so much at a time. Birds can carry only one twig at a time while building their nests, carry only one worm at a time to feed their babies, take care of only the most important, most urgent task at a time. This keeps them focused. Their priorities are right in order because they can do no differently.

I, on the other hand, become overly concerned and anxious because I overload every area of my life. I overdo and overindulge my schedule...my budget...my nerves...my strength...my expectations. I seem to stay in a perpetual state of anxiety, whereas birds do only what they can, day by day, little by little, in complete and total dependence upon their loving heavenly Father.

No wonder the birds sing their little hearts out!

They sing because they're happy.
They sing because they're free.
For His eye is on the sparrow.
And I know he watches me.[1]

Suddenly Jessie began to bark, alerting me that a car had just come up the drive. The children were home.

With a much lighter and very grateful heart, I pulled myself out of my reverie and my rocker and went to greet them while the ducks, ever hopeful, began to waddle once again toward the dog's dish.

1. ADAPTED FROM "HIS EYE IS ON THE SPARROW" BY CIVILLA D. MARTIN

ON THE WINNING SIDE

CHARLOTTE ADELSPERGER

My surgeon silently appeared at the bedside while I tried to focus on a large wall clock in the hospital recovery room. Without preface, he gave the biopsy report: "It was cancer." He went on: "I think you can keep your breast, but you have a long road ahead of you." He explained possible treatments, and tears stung my eyes. I began to tremble.

Then he squeezed my hand. "We can talk later," he said, and he slipped from the room.

I grasped for some kind of strength and familiar words surfaced from my memory:

"Fear not, for I am with you, be not dismayed, for I am your God; I will strengthen you, I will help you, I will uphold you with my victorious right hand." (Isaiah 41:10, RSV). I sensed God holding me, quieting my fear as only he can.

The nurse who helped me to the car after I was released did her best to be cheerful. My husband, Bob, sat very still behind the wheel, his face ashen. I felt a tremendous love for him. Then he took me into his arms and held me for a while before we started for home.

I had been one of those healthy women in her late forties, never concerned about the dreaded disease breast cancer. Then in April 1987, I was admitted to the hospital for a lumpectomy—removal of the tumor and surrounding tissue. Eighteen lymph nodes were removed from under my arm to find out how far the cancer had spread.

Part of my radiation treatment required isolation in a private room. Visitors could stay briefly but they had to sit behind a portable shield. Bob, with his usual humor, created a triangular yellow warning sign and hung it over my bed: "Radioactive Woman Aboard."

This was a time of draining pain and anxiousness. I kept my focus on God, our source of healing. I knew that trusting him was the only way to combat the fear. Then, just a few days after the surgery, my doctor had good news: The disease had not spread, and I would not have to go through chemotherapy. I smiled with relief, but I also knew that wasn't the end of the journey to healing and strength.

Fourteen days later I began daily trips to the hospital for localized radiation therapy. I had to stay still for each X-ray treatment, so to keep my mind from focusing on the disease or the tedium, I thought of words from Scripture or hymns. During those five weeks, I saw many people coming in for treatments. We who went daily got to know each other. Some of us were not terribly sick, but others were obviously very ill. What we shared, however, was a common enemy and a common fight. *We are in this together—we are a team,* I thought. As time went on, we talked more, cheered each other on, and promised to pray. Victory sang from deeper within me when I sang the song with others.

It was not always progress and healing, however. Treatments for cancer result in many painful side effects. When I started to experience radiation burns, it took all the support from other teammates—my husband, my third grade class, my friends both old and new—to help me with the struggle.

Twelve years later, I recognize more than ever that we are all *team* survivors. Whether the common enemy is disease, discouragement, or any other difficulty we face, God has given us each other for support along the way. Many women with cancer have opened their struggles and fears to me over the years. I started to keep an index card for each, noting the steps of her journey. Reading through them as I pray, I realize one thing: No matter how serious one's condition or situation may look, it is *together* that we affirm our hope and faith in God to take us through it.

My love for camaraderie continues; it is a gift God has given to his children. My husband, Bob, and I have walked with thousands of others in our local Susan G. Koman Breast Cancer Foundation Race for the Cure. Hundreds of survivors in pink T-shirts and caps run or walk in hope—and in victory. *We are in this together—we are a team.* It's an inspiring picture of how God intends his people to pull together.

The first year I participated in the Race for the Cure gave me a vivid picture of how God sees our struggles. As I approached the finish line, a deep-voiced announcer bellowed over the loud speaker: "Here comes another survivor! Let's bring her in!" Then came pounding applause, waves, and cheers. It reminded me that when we reach heaven it is God himself who stands at the end of our race, shouting in victory, "Here comes another who persevered! Bring her in!"

At the end of that race, a volunteer presented me with a pink rose. Tears sprang from my eyes—tears of thanks from the depth of my soul to the living God who has given me victory.

Restless

Because God has made us for Himself,
our hearts are restless until they rest in Him.

—SAINT AUGUSTINE

TWO BABES IN A MANGER

AUTHOR UNKNOWN

In 1994, two Americans answered an invitation from the Russian Department of Education to teach morals and ethics (based on biblical principles) in the public schools. They were invited to teach at prisons, businesses, the fire and police departments, and a large orphanage. About one hundred boys and girls who had been abandoned, abused, and left in the care of a government-run program were in the orphanage. They relate the following story in their own words:

It was nearing the holiday season, 1994. Time for our orphans to hear, for the first time, the traditional story of Mary and Joseph arriving in Bethlehem. Finding no room in the inn, the couple went to a stable, where the baby Jesus was born and placed in a manger.

Throughout the story, the children and orphanage staff sat in amazement as they listened.

Some sat on the edges of their stools, trying to grasp every word.

Completing the story, we gave the children three small pieces of cardboard to make a crude manger.

Each child was given a small paper square, cut from yellow napkins I had brought with me. No colored paper was available in the city. Following the instructions, the children tore the paper and carefully laid strips in the manger for straw. Small squares of flannel, cut from a worn-out nightgown an American lady threw away as she left Russia, were used for the baby's blankets. A doll-like baby was cut from tan felt we had brought from the United States. The orphans were busy assembling their mangers as I walked among them to see if they needed any help. All went well until I got to one table where little Misha sat. He looked to be about six years old and had finished his project.

As I looked at the little boy's manger, I was startled to see not one, but two babies in the manger. Quickly, I called for the translator to ask the lad why there were two babies in the manger. Crossing his arms in front of him and looking at this completed manger scene, the child began to repeat the story very seriously. For such a young child, who had only heard the Christmas story once, he related the happenings very accurately, until he came to the part where Mary put the baby Jesus in the manger.

Then Misha started to ad-lib. He made up his own ending to the story as he said, "And when Maria laid the baby in the manger, Jesus looked at me and asked me if I had a place to stay. I told him I have no mamma and I have no papa, so I don't have any place to stay. Then Jesus told me I could stay with him. But I told him I couldn't, because I didn't have a gift to give him like everybody else did. But I wanted to stay with Jesus so much, so I thought about what I had that maybe I could use for a gift. I thought maybe if I kept him warm, that would be a good gift. So I asked Jesus, 'If I keep you warm, will that be a good enough gift?'

"And Jesus told me, 'If you keep me warm, that will be the best gift anybody ever gave me.' So I got in the manger, and then Jesus looked at me and he told me that I could stay with him—for always."

As little Misha finished his story, his eyes brimmed full of tears that splashed down his little cheeks. Putting his hand over his face, his head dropped to the table and his shoulders shook as he sobbed and sobbed. The little orphan had found someone who would never abandon nor abuse him, someone who would stay with him—FOR ALWAYS.

For I am convinced that neither death nor life, neither angels nor demons, neither the present nor the future, nor any powers, neither height nor depth, nor anything else in all creation, will be able to separate us from the love of God that is in Christ Jesus our Lord.

ROMANS 8:38–39

THE KITCHEN TABLE

PHILIP GULLEY
FROM *FRONT PORCH TALES*

y hobby is woodworking and has been for a number of years. My foray into wood began when we needed a kitchen table and my wife suggested I build one. We were low on money, and I was between college and graduate school and had the time. I'd never built anything before, but a kitchen table seemed as good a place to start as any.

My grandfather had a workshop set up in the family barn. I'd go there in the morning, turn on the heater, and walk around sniffing the workshop odors. Grandpa had lubricated the drill press once a month since 1950, and I could smell nearly forty years of oil buildup in the corner where it sat. Over by the table saw I smelled sawdust. After a while I became a sawdust connoisseur and could tell the difference between pine sawdust and cherry sawdust. There are few scents more pleasant. The dog slept in the workshop, and I could smell her, too, wet and stagnant, like the pond used to smell with its August coat of scum.

It took me the month of February to build the table. I could have done it quicker, but being tucked away in the barn while winter blasted away outside was so pleasant it made me want to dwell on that page as long as I could. In March, I took the table outside beneath the trees, next to the crocuses that were pushing up, and sanded it down. Grandpa came by and taught me how to use slivers of glass to plane the joints smooth. That's an old woodworker's trick I never would have picked up on my own.

I spent a week massaging five coats of tung oil into the wood. It takes a long time to get the finish right on a piece of furniture, but you can't hurry it, or the flaws will show, and all your hard work will be for nothing. Woodworking is a good way to learn that doing something worthwhile takes time. It is possible to make a table in a hurry. It is not possible, however, to make a table worth passing on to your grandchildren in a hurry.

My wife and I wrapped the table in blankets, loaded it up in the truck, and carried it home. She gave me a brass plate, engraved with my name and the year, to mount on its underbelly. That's so when my children's children play underneath it, they'll be able to see when Grandpa built it.

I wanted to buy chairs to match, but we didn't have the money so we made do. Though every time we'd go into an antique store, we'd keep our eyes peeled. I even thought about making chairs, but building a good chair is extraordinarily difficult and time-consuming. I could build a bad chair in a day. After six years of haunting antique stores, we found four chairs. By then, times were better, and we took them home. Each is as fine a chair as can be had, and I intend to enjoy myriad ears of July sweet corn while sitting in them.

A friend came for dinner not long ago. He asked me where I had bought my table, and I told him I had made it. He wanted me to make him one, but I told him no. A man has to be careful not to let his hobby become his business. He was talking about how his kitchen table is forever falling apart and lamenting the shoddy nature of today's craftsmanship. People slapping things together in five minutes expecting them to last a lifetime.

We got to talking about how that isn't only true about furniture, it's true about life. Folks get discouraged because God doesn't make them saints overnight. They don't understand all the years of God-work that go into making one's life a thing of beauty— a lot of shaping, a lot of smoothing, a lot of finishing. And if we rush the process, the flaws will surely show.

Once a week I rub a coat of lemon oil into my table. It reminds me that my table is never really finished. Kind of like me.

Being confident of this, that he who began a good work in you will carry it on to completion until the day of Christ Jesus.

PHILIPPIANS 1:6

NOW PLAYING:

Sunrise over the Lake

Celestial nightlights adorn
the open theatre of predawn sky;
the moon rolls out its golden carpet
across the placid lake below.
The lights dim—
wind holds its breath
as the velvet curtain of night
begins its slow ascent.
From eastern wings, pale streaks of dawn
give hue and shape to the set;
thin shadows frame silhouettes
of characters and scenery.
The hush deepens…
finally broken by the first trills
of one lone robin
warming up for the overture.
The stage is set;
the cast awaits its cue—
the author nods and smiles,
then bids the day begin.

—ANN CAMPSHURE

GOD'S IN MY BASKET

CHRISTOPHER DE VINCK
FROM *SIMPLE WONDERS*

When I was in high school, my class was supposed to write a paper about someone over sev-
enty. I didn't know anyone over seventy except for my grandparents, but
they were living in Belgium. Then I thought: *I'll visit a nursing home and
ask permission to meet someone for my English assignment.*

When I entered the brick building, I walked up to the front desk. A
kind woman with glasses sent me to the director's office.

After I explained my assignment to the director, she sent me to room six.

Room six had a bed, a single chair, a desk, and a single picture of a
rose on the wall. Sitting in the chair was Mrs. Murphy. She was bent over,
knitting diligently. Her needles clicked and ticked. When I knocked on
her door, Mrs. Murphy looked up from her knitting and squinted.

"Yes?" she asked.

"I'm from the high school. I'm supposed to write an essay about
someone over seventy."

"Step out of the hall light. Come in. Come in." Mrs. Murphy stopped
knitting and patted the bed beside her. "Sit here."

I slowly entered the room, which smelled like lemon candy. I sat on
the left back corner of the little bed.

Mrs. Murphy returned to her knitting.

"What are you making?" I asked.

"God's in my basket," she answered.

Because I thought that she wasn't very good at hearing, I spoke a bit louder.

"What's in your basket, Mrs. Murphy?"

She stopped knitting again, turned her face in my direction, smiled, and repeated, "God's in my basket."

I looked around the room and finally noticed her knitting basket at the foot of her chair. It was filled with various balls of wool. I leaned forward to get a small peek in case I might catch a glimpse of God.

"Oh, he's there." Mrs. Murphy smiled.

"How can you tell?" I asked.

"I've prayed for him to come, and he has." With that, Mrs. Murphy returned to her basket and didn't say a word after that. No matter what I asked, she just continued rocking, smiling, and rocking some more.

Finally I stood up, thanked the old woman, and walked back into the bright hall light. Just before I left the building, the director stepped out from another room. She asked me how things went.

"Not so well," I said with disappointment. After all, my writing project was a failure. "She thinks that God is in her knitting basket."

"What's your name?" the woman asked.

"Christopher."

"That means *Christ bearer,* doesn't it?" she asked, more a statement of fact than a question to be verified. "What did you think of Mrs. Murphy?"

"I think she was a little crazy."

"She was when she first arrived," the director said. "When her husband died, she was alone. They didn't have any children. She has no family. She is ninety-three. All she wanted to do was die. That was five years ago. Then she said that all she wanted was peace. I suggested that she pray for peace. So that is what she did.

"A few months later she discovered knitting. A woman who came to us for a recreation hour taught Mrs. Murphy how to knit. In six months she was knitting socks for everyone. At the Christmas fair she sold over a thousand dollars worth of socks, wool dolls, sweaters, and blankets. She taught knitting in the local grade school as a volunteer. The children from the school would invite her home for dinner at least three times a week. Mrs. Murphy was the most popular person in our neighborhood and in our nursing home. She was truly happy."

"But what about now?" I asked.

"Well, she no longer remembers very much. She has become so old and sick, she has forgotten everyone's name."

"But she can still knit," I said.

"Yes, Christopher, she can still knit, and she is at peace. And something besides—she says only one sentence."

"God's in her basket."

"Yes, the God of peace."

I never did write my essay for school, but two weeks later a brown package waited for me at home. Inside I found a beautiful brown wool sweater just my size. I also found a note in a small white envelope:

Dear Christopher:

Mrs. Murphy asked that we send you this gift. She thought you'd like a bit of God to keep you warm. Mrs. Murphy died three days ago. She was very happy. Stop by and visit us again someday.

Sincerely,
Sister Claire

Do not be anxious about anything, but in everything, by prayer and petition, with thanksgiving, present your requests to God. And the peace of God, which transcends all understanding, will guard your hearts and your minds in Christ Jesus.

PHILIPPIANS 4:6–7

BETTER THAN I THOUGHT

BY RUTH BELL GRAHAM
FROM *A QUEST FOR SERENITY*

The story is told of a certain Italian painter who lost some of his artistic skill as he grew older. One evening he sat discouraged before a canvas he had just completed. He was painfully aware that it didn't burst with life as had his former paintings. As he climbed the stairs to bed, his son heard him mumbling to himself, "I have failed. I have failed."

Later that evening the son, also an artist, went into the studio to look at his father's painting. He, too, noticed that something was missing. Taking a palette and brush, he set to work, adding a touch of color here, a shadow there, a few highlights, greater depth. He continued far into the night, until at last the canvas fulfilled the old master's vision.

When morning came, the aging artist entered the studio to examine the work once again. He stood amazed before the perfected canvas and exclaimed in utter delight, "Ah, I have wrought better than I thought!"

The day will come when we will look upon the canvas of our lives and through the transforming power of Christ—a few shadows, a bit of color, dramatic highlights, added depth—we will be amazed to discover that we too fulfill our Heavenly Father's original vision.

As Jesus steps up and presents each of us, faultless, before his throne, and we hear the Father's, "Well done, thou good and faithful servant," we, too, will exclaim with utter joy, "Ah, I have wrought far better that I thought!"

Take heart! Remember…it is not about us, but about his glory.

A BALONEY SANDWICH

BOB BENSON
FROM *SEE YOU AT THE HOUSE*

*D*o you remember when they had old-fashioned Sunday school picnics? I do. As I recall, it was back in the "olden days," as my kids would say, back before they had air conditioning.

They said, "We'll all meet at the Sycamore Lodge in Shelby Park at four-thirty on Saturday. You bring your supper, and we'll furnish the iced tea."

But if you were like me, you came home at the last minute. When you got ready to pack your picnic, all you could find in the refrigerator was one dried up piece of baloney and just enough mustard in the bottom of the jar so that you got it all over your knuckles trying to get to it. And just two slices of stale bread to go with it. So you made your baloney sandwich and wrapped it in an old brown bag and went to the picnic.

When it came time to eat, you sat at the end of the table and spread out your sandwich. But the folks who sat next to you brought a feast. The lady was a good cook and she had worked hard all day to get ready for the picnic. And she had fried chicken and baked beans and potato salad and homemade rolls and sliced tomatoes and pickles and olives and celery. And two big homemade chocolate pies to top it off. That's what they spread out there next to you while you sat with your baloney sandwich.

But they said to you, "Why don't we just put it all together?"

"No, I couldn't do that. I couldn't even think of it," you murmured in embarrassment, with one eye on the chicken.

"Oh, come on, there's plenty of chicken and plenty of pie and plenty of everything. And we just love baloney sandwiches. Let's just put it all together."

And so you did and there you sat, eating like a king when you came like a pauper.

One day, it dawned on me that God had been saying that sort of thing to me. "Why don't you take what you have and what you are, and I will take what I have and what I am, and we'll share it together." I began to see that when I put what I had and was and am and hope to be with what He is, I had stumbled upon the bargain of a lifetime.

I get to thinking sometimes, thinking of me sharing with God. When I think of how little I bring, and how much He brings and invites me to share, I know that I should be shouting to the housetops, but I am so filled with awe and wonder that I can hardly speak. I know that I don't have enough love or faith or grace or mercy or wisdom, but He does. He has all of those things in abundance, and He says, "Let's just put it all together."

Consecration, denial, sacrifice, commitment, crosses—were all kind of hard words to me, until I saw them in the light of sharing. It isn't just a case of me kicking in what I have because God is the biggest kid in the neighborhood and He wants it all for Himself. He is saying, "Everything that I possess is available to you. Everything that I am and can be to a person, I will be to you."

When I think about it like that, it really amuses me to see somebody running along through life hanging on to their dumb bag with that stale baloney sandwich in it saying, "God's not going to get my sandwich! No, siree, this is mine!" Did you ever see anybody like that—so needy—just about half-starved to death, yet hanging on for dear life. It's not that God needs your sandwich. That fact is, you need His chicken!

Well, go ahead—eat your baloney sandwich, as long as you can. But when you can't stand its tastelessness or drabness any longer; when you get so tired of running your own life by yourself and doing it your way and figuring out all the answers with no one to help; when trying to accumulate, hold, grasp, and keep everything together in your own strength gets to be too big a load; when you begin to realize that by yourself you're never going to be able to fulfill your dreams, I hope you'll remember that it doesn't have to be that way.

You have been invited to something better, you know. You have been invited to share in the very being of God.

Prayer

OTHERS

Lord, help me live from day to day
In such a self-forgetful way,
That even when I kneel to pray,
My prayer may be for others.

—Henry Wadsworth Longfellow

TIMMY

HOWARD HENDRICKS
FROM *SAY IT WITH LOVE*

We knew a lovely couple in Dallas a number of years ago. He sold his business at a loss, went into vocational Christian work, and things got rather rough. There were four kids in the family. One night at family worship, Timmy, the youngest boy, said, "Daddy, do you think Jesus would mind if I asked Him for a shirt?"

"Well, no, of course not. Let's write that down in our prayer request book, Mother."

So she wrote down "shirt for Timmy" and she added "size seven." You can be sure that every day Timmy saw to it that they prayed for the shirt. One Saturday the mother received a telephone call from a clothier in downtown Dallas, a Christian businessman. "I've finished my July clearance sale and knowing that you have four boys it occurred to me that you might use something we have left. Could you use some boys' shirts?"

She said, "What size?"

"Size seven."

"How many do you have?" she asked hesitantly.

He said, "Twelve."

Many of us might have taken the shirts, stuffed them in the bureau drawer, and made some casual comment to the children. Not this wise set of parents. That night, as expected, Timmy said, "Don't forget, Mommy, let's pray for the shirt."

Mommy said, "We don't have to pray for the shirt, Timmy."

"How come?"

"The Lord has answered our prayer."

"He has?"

"Right." So, as previously arranged, brother Tommy goes out and gets one shirt, brings it in, and puts it down on the table. Little Timmy's eyes are like saucers. Tommy goes out and gets another shirt and brings it in. Out, back, out, back, until he piles twelve shirts on the table, and Timmy thinks God is going into the shirt business. But you know, there is a little kid in Dallas today by the name of Timothy who believes there is a God in heaven interested enough in his needs to provide boys with shirts.

Different Answers

They're almost unbelievable—
some prayer answers
You sent so fast
they took my breath away
And made me laugh.
I thank You.

I thank You there were other times
it seemed
You've left me
way out
in the dark
alone
to wait…
Until You became
more important
than any answer
I was looking for.

—Nancy Spiegelberg
From *Fanfare*

FIRST PRAYER

JOHN WILLSEA

Today I observed my two-year-old son pray his first prayer. Wesley folded his hands, bowed his head over his lunch and said, "Dear Jesus, welcome." He often says "welcome" for "thank you." In the midst of a day that I felt like a failure as a parent, this ray of sunshine broke through my gloom. What my child gave thanks for, I had failed to do. Lord, in the commonplace, in the everyday, help me to echo Wesley's prayer: Dear Jesus, welcome.

LETTERS TO A STRANGER

SUSAN MORIN
FROM *THE CHRISTIAN READER*

t was a bitter January evening in 1992 when the phone rang and my fifteen-year-old son Tajin hollered, "Mom, it's for you!"

"Who is it?" I asked. I was tired. It had been a long day. In fact, it had been a long month. The engine in my car died five days before Christmas, and I had just returned to work after being out with the flu. I was feeling overwhelmed having to purchase another vehicle and having lost a week's pay due to illness. There seemed to be a cloud of despair hanging over my heart.

"It's Bob Thompson," Tajin answered.

The name didn't register. As I walked over to pick up the phone, the last name seemed vaguely familiar. *Thompson...Bob Thompson...Thompson?* Like a computer searching for the right path, my mind finally made the connection. *Beverly Thompson.* In the brief time it took me to reach the phone, my mind replayed the last nine months.

As I drove to work last March, some patches of snow were still on the ground, but the river, winding on my left, had opened up and was full of swift-moving water. The warm sun coming through my windshield seemed to give hope of an early spring.

The winter of 1991 had been a hard one for me as a single working mother. The three children were in their teens, and I was finding it hard to cope both with their changing emotional needs and our financial needs. Each month I struggled to provide the bare necessities.

I faithfully attended church and a Bible study but had very little time for anything else. I longed to serve the Lord in a way that had some significance. So that day I again apologized to him that I had so little to give back to him. It seemed I was always asking him to meet my needs or answer my prayers.

"Lord, what can I do for you? I feel like I'm always taking from you because my needs are so great." The answer to my own question seemed so simple. Prayer.

"Okay, Lord, I will commit this time that I have during my drive to work to prayer. Will you give me some people to pray for? I don't even have to know their needs, just let me know who they are." My heart lifted as I continued to speak to him during the remainder of my forty-five minute trip from New Hampshire to Vermont.

I arrived at work and proceeded to open the mail and prepare the deposit. I was in charge of accounts receivable for the Mary Meyer Corporation, a company that makes stuffed animals. I opened one envelope and attached to the check was a note that said, "I'm sorry this payment is late. I have been seriously ill. Thank you, Beverly Thompson."

I can't explain it, but I instantly knew that this was the person the Lord had given me to pray for. "You want me to pray for her, don't you, Lord?" I asked him silently. The answer came in a feeling of peace and excitement combined—I knew he had just answered my prayer from less than an hour ago!

So began my journey of prayer for Beverly Thompson. At first I found it very awkward to pray for someone I didn't even know. I did know one thing besides her name. She owned Chapter 1 Bookstore in Presque Isle, Maine, and she ordered bulk quantities of our plush animals to sell. I didn't know how old she was. Was she married, widowed, single, or divorced? What was wrong with her? Was it terminal? Did she have any children?

The answers to these questions weren't revealed as I prayed for Beverly, but I did find out how much the Lord loved her and that she was not forgotten by him. Many days I would find myself in tears as I entered into prayer for her. I prayed that he would give her comfort for whatever she would have to endure. Or I pled for strength and courage for her to accept things that she might find hard to face.

One morning, as my wipers pushed the spring rain off my windshield, I saw muted tones of browns and greys. I prayed that the Lord would give Beverly eyes to see that the same drab landscape could be transformed into the greens and yellows of spring by a single day filled with sunshine. I prayed she could find hope even though it might seem covered up in the muted tones of her life and rely on God who can transform winter into spring.

In May, I felt that I should send her a card to let her know I was praying for her. As I made this decision, I knew I was taking a risk. Because I had taken her name from where I worked, I could possibly lose my job. I wasn't in a position to be without any income.

But, God, I told him, *I've grown to love Beverly Thompson. I know you'll take care of me no matter what happens.* In my first card, I told Beverly a little bit about myself and how I had asked the Lord for specific people to pray for. Then I mentioned how I had come to get her name. I also told her that the Lord knew all about what she was going through and wanted her to know how much he loved her.

I certainly knew how much God loved me. When I first moved into this new town, it had been difficult, especially as a single mom. But only a few weeks after arriving, I bought a Bible for fifty cents at a yard sale. When I got home, I found a folded note inside.

When I opened it, I couldn't believe my eyes.

"Dear Susan," the handwritten note began, "'he who began a good work in you will carry it on to completion until the day of Christ Jesus' (Philippians1:6)." Obviously, the writer was encouraging another Susan, since I had randomly picked up the Bible. But for me, it was assurance

God was personally interested in me!

Summer came and went, and I continued to send Beverly cards and notes. I never heard from her, but I never stopped praying for her, even telling my Tuesday night Bible study group the story. They also upheld her in prayer.

At times I had to admit to God that I really wanted a response; I wanted to know what Beverly thought about this stranger and her steady stream of notes. Did she think I was completely crazy? Did she hope I'd stop?

I took the phone from my son's hand and immediately my hand went clammy. *I know why he's calling. He's calling me to tell me to stop bothering his wife. They probably think I'm a religious kook.* A million scenarios flew through my mind.

"Hello, Mr. Thompson," my voice squeaked nervously.

"My daughter Susan and I have just been going through my wife's things and found your cards and notes and your phone number. We wanted to call and let you know how much they meant to Beverly and to fill you in on what happened."

My heart loosened as this grieving husband continued to tell me about Beverly's last days.

"While we were going through her things, we found your cards and notes tied up with a red ribbon. I know she must have read them over and over because they looked worn."

Then he said quietly, "My wife had been diagnosed with lung cancer at the age of forty-eight."

I winced at the thought of Beverly's physical setback, but Mr. Thompson's next words comforted me. "She never suffered any pain at all. I know that this was a result of your prayers."

Then he answered one of the questions I had nagged God about. "The reason you never heard back from her was because she also developed brain cancer," he said.

"Our relationship with God amounted to going to church once in a while, but it was nothing that had much effect on our lives," Mr. Thompson explained. "I wanted you to know that my wife asked to be baptized two weeks before she passed away. The night before she died she told me it was okay for her to die because she was going home to be with her Lord."

As Bob Thompson continued to share his wife's story with me, the drab landscape of my own life was transformed. As insignificant as my life had appeared to be to me, God used it to shine his love upon another life, resulting in a gift that no one could take away.

The experience increased my faith significantly. God took one of the lowest points in my life and added glints of his glory. It made me realize that when we're willing to be obedient, God works in profound ways.

A SMALL GIRL'S PRAYER

HELEN ROSEVEARE
FROM *UNSOLVED MIRACLES*

ne night I had worked hard to help a mother in the labor ward; but in spite of all we could do, she died, leaving us with a tiny premature baby and a crying two-year-old daughter. We would have difficulty keeping the baby alive, as we had no incubator (we had no electricity to run an incubator!) and no special feeding facilities. Although we lived on the equator, nights were often chilly with treacherous drafts. One student midwife went for the box we had for such babies and the cotton wool the baby would be wrapped in. Another went to stoke up the fire and fill a hot water bottle. She came back shortly; in distress, to tell me that in filling the bottle, it had burst. Rubber perishes easily in tropical climates.

"And it is our last hot water bottle!" she exclaimed.

As in the West it is no good crying over spilled milk, so in Central Africa it might be considered no good crying over burst water bottles. They do not grow on trees, and there are no drugstores down forest pathways.

"All right," I said. "Put the baby as near the fire as you safely can; sleep between the baby and the door to keep it free from drafts. Your job is to keep the baby warm."

The following noon, as I did most days, I went to have prayers with any of the orphanage children who chose to gather with me. I gave the youngsters various suggestions of things to pray about and told them about the tiny baby. I explained our problem about keeping the baby warm enough, mentioning the hot water bottle. The baby could so easily die if it got chills. I also told them of the two-year-old sister, crying because her mother had died.

During the prayer time, one ten-year-old girl, Ruth, prayed with the usual blunt conciseness of our African children.

"Please, God," she prayed, "send us a water bottle. It'll be no good tomorrow, God, as the baby'll be dead, so please send it this afternoon."

While I gasped inwardly at the audacity of the prayer, she added by way of corollary; "And while You are about it, would You please send a dolly for the little girl so she'll know You really love her?"

As often with children's prayers, I was put on the spot. Could I honestly say "Amen"? I just did not believe that God could do this. Oh, yes, I know that He can do everything. The Bible says so. But there are limits, aren't there? And I had some very big "buts." The only way God could answer this particular prayer would be by sending me a parcel from the homeland. I had been in Africa for almost four years at that time, and I had never, ever received a parcel from home; anyway if anyone did send me a parcel, who would put in a hot water bottle? I lived on the equator!

Halfway through the afternoon, while I was teaching in the nurses' training school, a message was sent that there was a car at my front door. By the time I reached home, the car had gone, but there, on the verandah, was a large twenty-two pound parcel. I felt tears pricking my eyes. I could not open the parcel alone, so I sent for the orphanage children. Together we pulled off the string, carefully undoing each knot. We folded the paper, taking care not to tear it unduly. Excitement was mounting. Some thirty or forty pairs of eyes were focused on the large cardboard box.

From the top, I lifted out brightly colored, knitted jerseys. Eyes sparkled as I gave them out. Then there were the knitted bandages for the leprosy patients, and the children looked a little bored! Then came a box of mixed raisins and sultanas—that would make a nice batch of buns for the weekend. Then, as I put my hand in again, I felt the…could it really be? I grasped it and pulled it out— yes, a brand-new, rubber hot water bottle!

I cried. I had not asked God to send it; I had not truly believed that He could.

Ruth was in the front row of the children. She rushed forward crying out, "If God has sent the bottle, He must have sent the dolly, too!"

Rummaging down to the bottom of the box, she pulled out the small, beautifully dressed dolly. Her eyes shone! She had never doubted.

Looking up at me, she asked: "Can I go over with you, Mummy, and give this dolly to that little girl, so she'll know that Jesus really loves her?"

That parcel had been on the way for five whole months. Packed up by my former Sunday school class, whose leader had heard and obeyed God's prompting to send a hot water bottle, even to the equator. And one of the girls had put in a dolly for an African child—five months before an answer to the believing prayer of a ten-year-old to bring it "that afternoon."

SECRET CODE

SARA ANN DUBOSE

"A code?" Bob asked.

"Sure, why not?" Sonny answered. "You ask the questions, and I'll knock out the answers on the telephone receiver. Look. If it's yes, I'll knock three times, and if it's no, I'll knock once, like this."

Sonny Paterson rapped the receiver.

"I can read you loud and clear," Bob said. "I'll call you Tuesday afternoon. Now, before we hang up, let's pray."

The prayer was short, but as Bob prayed, Sonny tried to commit the next few days to God. The flight from Montgomery to Houston would take no longer than the surgery; about three hours. But coming out of the operating room, Sonny would be minus a voice box. His communication would be cut to a knock, a nod, or a piece of paper and pencil. Later, Sonny might want special laryngcal speech lessons, but for now his one objective was to have the Texas surgeon cut his cancer away.

"Amen," Bob said.

"Amen," Sonny replied. "I'll be waiting to hear from you on Tuesday."

Sonny Paterson— a prominent Montgomery businessman, an active layman in the church— had only three more days to talk. How could he speak everything on his mind? How could he tell his wife and family how much they meant to him? There would still be communication, but what if he couldn't learn the tricky speech method the physician described? The doctor would have a voice box, not a funny hole in the middle of his throat.

Sonny tried to shut off the pessimism. He'd had troubles before, and God had never let him down. At the same time, Sonny knew full well that a person's heart can accept and trust something, while his mind and body still want to rebel.

Tuesday came. The papers were in order. Blood pressure, temperature, pulse—all checked and found normal. Waiting, saying good-bye, rolling, then nothing until waking up with a dry, hollow feeling of having something missing. Smiles, handholding. It was over, the offending cancer removed.

The ring came later. Sonny checked his watch and reached for the phone. It was five o'clock.

"Sonny? Bob Strong. Is it all over?"

Knock, knock, knock, came the reply.

"Are you in much pain?"

Knock.

"Sonny, I have one more question. Has God stood with you? Have you felt His grace through all this?"

There was a pause, and then it started. Not once, not three times, but again and again and again and again until Bob Strong finally closed the conversation with another loud, "Amen."

Let us then approach the throne of grace with confidence,
so that we may receive
mercy and find grace to help us in our time of need.

HEBREWS 4:16

NIGHTTIME PRAYERS

ALICE GRAY

The little boy was saying his bedtime prayers as he had done every night with his dad kneeling beside him. He started with,

"Now I lay me down to sleep, I pray the Lord my soul to keep."

Part way through the little boy got mixed up.

"If I should wake before I die…"

Realizing his mistake the little boy stopped mid-sentence, looked up at his dad, and then started to say the prayer over from the beginning. The father tenderly put his arm around his son's small shoulders and said, "That's okay. It's probably the first time that prayer has been said right. For it is my greatest desire that you will wake before you die— wake to the truth of knowing Jesus Christ as your Lord and Savior."

WALKING BY FAITH

CHARLES R. SWINDOLL
FROM *THE STRONG FAMILY*

My wife and I dearly love a particular family…a mom and dad and *seven* kids. Not long ago they told us of a period of time in their earlier years as a family when they were forced to trust God through some unusual circumstances. At that time in their lives they were financially strapped. They literally didn't have another meal to put on the table! That morning their dad prayed with them as the mother scraped together the last bit of flour and milk to bake them biscuits. After they ate them, the dad said to the family before he left that morning to work as a carpenter: "Children, God must provide for us today. This is absolutely all we have to eat. But He loves us dearly. We are going to trust Him to provide for our needs." I doubt that the children even had lunches that day to take with them to school. We're talking zero.

Later that morning a friend happened to drop by and said, "I understand that Dave is now working as a carpenter."

"Well, yes, that's true," said Kaya, his wife.

They chatted briefly, and before Kaya knew it, the lady started hauling in bags and bags of groceries. By the time the friend finished, there were bags loaded with food stacked all over the kitchen counter—even a little bag of Oreo cookies poking from the top of the last bag.

Dumbfounded, yet full of tearful gratitude, Kaya told the visitor what had occurred during their morning time of prayer with the family—how she was a direct answer to prayer. The woman, of course, had no idea. The Lord had just prompted her to carry out that mission of mercy. She was extra thrilled. Well, Kaya had the joy of filling up their shelves with groceries. What an amazing provision! Finally, she put the Oreo cookies in a special cookie jar and sat it on the counter, knowing her family's love for Oreos.

When Dave came tooling in that evening, he saw the jar stuffed with cookies and said, "Good night, Kaya...we only have a little bit and you just bought all these Oreo cookies?"

She replied, "No, Dave, *not a little bit*." And with grand gestures, she opened the pantry and displayed shelf after shelf of groceries. Guess whose kids understand the excitement of walking by faith?

The earnest prayer of a righteous man
has great power and wonderful results.

JAMES 5:16, THE LIVING BIBLE

Crosses

Dear God,
Give me strength to bear the crosses
that are large enough for all to see…
But also give me strength to bear the crosses
that are known only to thee and me.

—PATRICIA NIELAND-COLLINS

A PLACE OF TAKING HOLD

JONI EARECKSON TADA
FROM *A QUIET PLACE IN A CRAZY WORLD*

I often pray for children around the world on the basis of God's tenderness and compassion toward boys and girls. I claim His love, and hold fast to the promise of who He is.

Even a casual look at the life of Jesus in Scripture shows how these attributes of His character bubbled up like water from an artesian well every time He was around a child. It was as if He could hardly contain Himself from blessing them, drawing them near, and honoring them with a "first place" status in the kingdom. If that's the way He was with children who ran up to Him, boys and girls who could walk and see and hear and use their hands, how much more His heart must have gone out to handicapped children.

It was good to cling to this picture of Jesus as I entered the Bucharest orphanage. Especially when they carried little Vasile into the room to meet me.

They said he was seven or eight; he looked like a frail three-year-old. They told us he was dying of colon cancer. I looked at him...tiny hands and feet...faint little voice...soft brown eyes, clouded with pain. He seemed weak from lack of nutrition. When they lifted up his little shirt to show me his distended abdomen, he winced in pain.

I asked for Vasile to be sat in my lap.

"Vasile," I said, "Have you ever ridden a bicycle?"

"No."

"Would you like to go for a ride in my wheelchair? Da?"

He nodded.

"I'll share my wheels with you, Vasile!"

We wheeled around and around the drab, cement floored room as a steady rain pattered against the windows.

A small smile crossed his face. I made up a song as we wheeled around in the colorless little room. "Vasile is your name, Vasile is your name."

"Do you know Jesus, Vasile? Do you know where Jesus lives? He lives in heaven. Would you like to be with Him in heaven?"

Vasile nodded his little head.

I prayed, "Dear Jesus, we love You, and we love how You love children. This little boy loves You, too. Take Him home to be with You, Jesus."

Mary Lance, one of our team's front-line, on-the-scene prayer warriors, prayed that if it was the Lord's will, that little Vasile might be healed.

I, too, prayed silently with all my heart: *Lord, You had compassion on the little children when You walked on earth, and You are the same today...may these handicapped children have power with You, feel Your closeness...may You meet their needs as You met the needs of the boys and girls whom You blessed with Your own hands.*

We based our prayers on the power of God's attributes. And the Lord heard our petitions. Vasile was spared. He did not have colon cancer after all, but a treatable disease. Today he has a family in Bakersfield, California. He is healthy and whole and full of little-boy mischief and smiles.

And he has his own bicycle.

The Spirit helps us in our weakness.
We do not know what we ought to pray,
but the Spirit himself intercedes for us
with groans that words cannot express.

ROMANS 8:26

Faith

FAITH IS...

Resting in His love,
His presence,
His provision.

—PAMELA REEVE
FROM *FAITH IS*

I'M HERE!

ROBERT STRAND
FROM *MOMENTS FOR MOTHERS*

The Rogers are devout Christians who have built a strong family. The father has a special interest in the spiritual condition of each of his children and often would quiz them in order to know if they were sure of their salvation. Occasionally he would ask them to share in their own words about their relationship with Jesus Christ.

One day it was seven-year-old Jimmy's turn to express how he knew he had eternal life. Jimmy told his version: "I think it will be something like this in heaven. One day when we all get to go to Heaven, it will be time for the big angel to read from the big book the names of all the people who will be there. He will come to the Rogers family and say, 'Daddy Rogers?' and Daddy will say, 'Here!' then the angel will call out 'Mommy Rogers?' and Mommy will say, 'Here!' Then the angel will come down to call out Susie Rogers and Mavis Rogers, and they will both say 'Here!'"

He paused, took a big deep breath and continued "And finally that big angel will read my name, Jimmy Rogers, and because I'm little and maybe he'll miss me, I'll jump and shout real loud, 'Here!' to make sure he knows I'm there."

Just a few days later there was a tragic accident. A car struck down little

Jimmy Rogers as he made his way to catch the school bus. He was rushed by ambulance to the hospital, and all the family was summoned. He was in critical condition.

The little family group gathered around the bed in which little Jimmy now lay with no movement, no consciousness, and no hope for recovery. The doctors had done all that was in their power. Jimmy would probably be gone by morning.

The family prayed and waited. Late in the night the little boy seemed to be stirring a bit. They all moved closer. They saw his lips move; just one word was all he uttered before he passed from this life. But what a word of comfort and hope for a grieving family he was to leave behind. In the clear voice of a little boy, loud and clear enough so all could hear and understand, little Jimmy Rogers said the one word:

"Here!"

And then he was gone.

THROUGH

BILLY GRAHAM
FROM *THE SECRETS OF HAPPINESS*

$\mathcal{I}$ saw a painting in England which showed a soldier who had gone to the front to repair the communications lines. The message which was to flow through those lines meant life to hundreds and perhaps thousands of men. He found a breach in the wires but had nothing with which to repair the break. While the enemy shells were bursting around him, he took one broken cable in his left hand and stretching his right hand grasped the other cable and made the connection. The dramatic picture had a one word title: "Through."

Christ, in His vicarious death on the cross, repaired the breach between God and man. The Bible says: "He is our peace" (Ephesians 2:14). Those who were afar off are made nigh…. He has made both one. *Through Him alone* we have peace!

THE FATHER'S ANGUISHING DECISION

CARLA MUIR

After a few of the usual Sunday evening hymns, the church's pastor once again slowly stood up, walked over to the pulpit, and gave a very brief introduction of his childhood friend. With that, an elderly man stepped up to the pulpit to speak. "A father, his son, and a friend of his son were sailing off the Pacific Coast," he began, "when a fast approaching storm blocked any attempt to get back to shore. The waves were so high, that even though the father was an experienced sailor, he could not keep the boat upright, and the three were swept into the ocean."

The old man hesitated for a moment, making eye contact with two teenagers who were, for the first time since the service began, looking somewhat interested in his story. He continued, "Grabbing a rescue line, the father had to make the most excruciating decision of his life...to which boy he would throw the other end of the line. He only had seconds to make the decision. The father knew that his son was a Christian, and he also knew that his son's friend was not. The agony of his decision could not be matched by the torrent of waves. As the father yelled out, 'I love you, son!' he threw the line to his son's friend. By the time he pulled the friend back to the capsized boat, his son had disappeared beyond the raging swells into the black of night. His body was never recovered."

By this time, the two teenagers were sitting straighter in the pew, waiting for the next words to come out of the old man's mouth. "The father," he continued, "knew his son would step into eternity with Jesus, and he could not bear the thought of his son's friend stepping into an eternity without Jesus. Therefore, he sacrificed his son. How great is the love of God that He should do the same for us." With that, the old man turned and sat back down in his chair as silence filled the room.

Within minutes after the service ended, the two teenagers were at the old man's side. "That was a nice story," politely started one of the boys, "but I don't think it was very realistic for a father to give up his son's life in hopes that the other boy would become a Christian."

"Well, you've got a point there," the old man replied, glancing down at his worn Bible. A big smile broadened his narrow face, and he once again looked up at the boys and said, "It sure isn't very realistic, is it? But I'm standing here today to tell you that *that* story gives me a glimpse of what it must have been like for God to give up his Son for me. You see…I was the son's friend."

Faith and Doubt

Doubt sees the obstacles,
Faith sees the way;
Doubt sees the blackest night,
Faith sees the day;
Doubt dreads to take a step,
Faith soars on high;
Doubt questions, "Who believes?"
Faith answers, "I."

—AUTHOR UNKNOWN

HEART SOUNDS

AUTHOR UNKNOWN

A nurse on the pediatric ward, before listening to the little ones' chests, would plug the stethoscope into their ears and let them listen to their own hearts. Their eyes would always light up with awe.

But she never got a response equal to four-year-old David's. Gently he tucked the stethoscope in his ears and placed the disk over his heart. "Listen," she said. "What do you suppose that is?"

He drew his eyebrows together in a puzzled line and looked as if lost in the mystery of the strange tap-tap-tapping deep in his chest. Then his face broke out in a wondrous grin. "Is that Jesus knocking?" he asked.

HER FAVORITE VERSE

RON MEHL
FROM *CURE FOR A TROUBLED HEART*

I heard once about a dear, saintly old woman who was gradually losing her memory. Details began to blur. Once-familiar names began to elude her, and finally, even well-loved faces slipped from recognition. Throughout her life, however, this woman had cherished and depended on the Word of God, committing to memory many verses from her worn King James Bible.

Her favorite verse had always been 2 Timothy 1:12:

> *For I know whom I have believed and am*
> *persuaded that he is able to keep that which*
> *I have committed unto him against that day.*

She was finally confined to bed in a nursing home, and her family knew she would never leave the bed alive. As they visited with her, she would still quote the verses of Scripture on occasion. Especially 2 Timothy 1:12. But with the passing of time, even parts of this well-loved verse began to slip away.

"I know whom I have believed," she would say. "He is able to keep...what I have committed...to him."

Her voice grew weaker. And the verse became even shorter. "What I have committed…to him."

As she was dying, her voice became so faint family members had to bend over and listen to the few whispered words on her lips. And at the end, there was only one word of her life verse left.

"Him."

She whispered it again and again as she stood on the threshold of heaven. "Him…Him…Him."

It was all that was left. It was all that was needed. She couldn't recall the verse, but the word she remembered was by far the most important word in the Bible. She held onto the one word that is really the heart of the Word…"Him."

REMINDER

LEROY BROWNLOW
FROM *A PSALM IN MY HEART*

Years ago a French infidel strutted and bragged that infidels would tear down the churches and destroy everything that reminded the people of God. A poor peasant replied, "But you will leave us the sun, the moon, and the stars; and as long as they shine, we shall have a reminder of God."

The heavens declare the glory of God;
the skies proclaim the work of his hands.
Day after day they pour forth speech;
night after night they display knowledge.
There is no speech or language where
their voice is not heard. Their
voice goes out into all the earth,
their words to the ends of the world.

PSALM 19:1–4

DOING WHAT
OUR FATHER SAYS

LUIS PALAU

FROM *HEALTHY HABITS FOR SPIRITUAL GROWTH*

More than ninety people conducted an all-night search for Dominic DeCarlo, an eight-year-old boy lost on a snowy mountain. Dominic, who had been on a skiing trip with his father, apparently had skied off the run without realizing it.

As each hour passed, the search party and the boy's family became more concerned. By dawn they had found no trace of the boy. Two helicopter crews joined the search, and within fifteen minutes they spotted ski tracks. A ground team followed the tracks, which changed to small footprints. The footprints led to a tree, where they found the boy.

"He's in super shape!" Sergeant Terry Silbaugh, area search-and-rescue coordinator, announced. "In fact, he's in better shape than we are right now!" A hospital spokeswoman said the boy was in fine condition, so he wasn't even admitted.

Silbaugh explained why the boy did so well despite spending a night in the freezing elements: His father had enough forethought to warn the boy about what to do if he became lost, and his son had enough trust to do exactly what his father said. As a young child, he never would have thought of snuggling up to a tree and covering himself with branches. He was simply obeying his wise and loving father.

Dominic reminds me of what we should do as children of our loving and infinitely wise heavenly Father. We are not to walk according to the course of this world, which is passing away. Instead, we are to walk in obedience to the Lord's commands because He knows what is best for us.

In a world full of deceptive detours and confusing paths, let's trust our Father and do exactly what He says.

Trust in the Lord with all your heart
and lean not on your own understanding;
in all your ways acknowledge him,
and he will make your paths straight.

PROVERBS 3:5–6

SAYING GOODBYE

BILLY GRAHAM
FROM *HOPE FOR THE TROUBLED HEART*

*H*e was just a little boy, only ten years old, but Russell Davis knew what it was to live a life of pain. For four years he fought a battle with cancer. One Saturday, when he was back in the hospital again, he wrote this note to his best friend:

> *Dear Brian,*
>
> *How are you doing? I'm alright in the hospital but a little sleepy. I know that you worry about me some but don't worry too much. Also if it will help you feel better you can come see me if you have time.*
> *When I die, if I do soon, don't worry 'cause I'll be somewhere special in Heaven. And sooner than I know it you'll be up in Heaven with me 'cause a thousand years on earth is a minute in Heaven.*
> *I know you'll miss me when I'm gone but just accept it like you did with your uncle. My mom will give you something of mine so you can remember me always. So don't worry too much.*
>
> *Love, Russell.*

Three days later, Russell asked for a sip of water and said, "I love you, Mom. I love you, Dad." And he went home to be with the Lord. Some people write better sermons when they die than others do in a lifetime of speaking.

THE SHEPHERD'S PSALM

ROBERT STRAND

FROM *ESPECIALLY FOR THE HURTING HEART*

There is a story of an old man and a young man on the same platform before an audience. A special part of the program was being presented. Each of the men was to repeat from memory the Twenty-Third Psalm. The young man, trained in speech and drama, gave in oratory, the Psalm. When finished the audience clapped for more so that they could hear his beautiful, modulated voice once more.

Then the old man, leaning on his cane, stepped to the front of the platform and in a feeble, shaking voice, repeated the same words. But when he was seated no sound came from the listeners.

Folks wiped tears as they seemed to pray. In the ensuing silence, the young man again stepped forward and made the following statement: "Friends, I wish to make an explanation. You asked me to repeat the Psalm with your applause, but you remained silent when my friend was finished. The difference? I shall tell you. I know the Psalm, but he knows the Shepherd of the Psalm."

The Lord Is My Shepherd

The Lord is my shepherd; I shall not want.

He maketh me to lie down in green pastures;

he leadeth me beside the still waters.

He restoreth my soul;

he leadeth me in the paths of righteousness for his name's sake.

Yea, though I walk through the valley of the shadow of death,

I will fear no evil; for thou art with me;

thy rod and thy staff they comfort me.

Thou preparest a table before me in the presence of mine enemies;

thou anointest my head with oil; my cup runneth over.

Surely goodness and mercy shall follow me all the days of my life;

and I will dwell in the house of the Lord forever.

PSALM 23, KING JAMES BIBLE

SOMEONE IS WAITING

AUTHOR UNKNOWN

John Todd was born in Rutledge, Vermont, into a family of several children. They later moved to the village of Killingsworth back in the early 1880s. There, at a very early age, both of John's parents died. One dear and loving aunt said she would take little John. The aunt sent a horse and servant, Caesar, to get John who was only six at this time. On the way back this endearing conversation took place.

John: Will she be there?

Caesar: Oh, yes, she'll be there waiting up for you.

John: Will I like living with her?

Caesar: My son, you fall into good hands.

John: Will she love me?

Caesar: Aye, she has a big heart.

John: Will I have my own room? Will she let me have a puppy?

Caesar: She's got everything all set, son. I think she has some surprises, John.

John: Do you think she'll go to bed before we get there?

Caesar: Oh, no! She'll be sure to wait up for you. You'll see when we get out of these woods. You'll see her candle in the window.

Sure enough, as they neared the house, John saw a candle in the window and his aunt standing in the doorway. As he shyly approached the porch, she reached down, kissed him, and said, "Welcome home!"

John Todd grew up in his aunt's home and later became a great minister. She was mother to him. She gave him a second home.

Years later his aunt wrote to tell John of her own impending death because of failing health. She wondered what would become of her.

This is what John Todd wrote in reply:

My Dear Aunt,

Years ago, I left a house of death, not knowing where I was to go, whether anyone cared, whether it was the end of me. The ride was long, but the servant encouraged me. Finally I arrived to your embrace and a new home. I was expected; I felt safe. You did it all for me.
Now it's your turn to go. I'm writing to let you know, someone is waiting up, your room is all ready, the light is on, the door is open, and you're expected! I know. I once saw God standing in your doorway...long ago!

I go to prepare a place for you.
And if I go and prepare a place for you,
I will come again and receive you to Myself;
that where I am, there you may be also.

JOHN 14:2–3, *NEW KING JAMES VERSION*

Autumn Reflections

*The water of life needs to be replenished,
the soul refreshed,
the weary head anointed,
the cup filled,
the feast eaten,
the spirit revived
in preparation for Winter—
and for the promise of Spring Eternal.*

—NOLA BERTELSON

THE ROOM

JOSHUA HARRIS
FROM *I KISSED DATING GOODBYE*

*I*n that place between wakefulness and dreams, I found myself in the room. There were no distinguishing features save for the one wall covered with small index-card files. They were like the ones in libraries that list titles by author or subject in alphabetical order. But these files, which stretched from floor to ceiling and seemingly endlessly in either direction, had very different headings. As I drew near the wall of files, the first to catch my attention was one that read "Girls I Have Liked." I opened it and began flipping through the cards. I quickly shut it, shocked to realize that I recognized the names written on each one.

And then without being told, I knew exactly where I was. This lifeless room with its small files was a crude catalog system for my life. Here were written the actions of my every moment, big and small, in a detail my memory couldn't match.

A sense of wonder and curiosity, coupled with horror, stirred within me as I began randomly opening files and exploring their contents. Some brought joy and sweet memories; others a sense of shame and regret so intense that I would look over my shoulder to see if anyone was watching. A file named "Friends" was next to one marked "Friends I Have Betrayed." The titles ranged from the mundane to the outright weird. "Books I Have Read," "Lies I Have Told," "Comfort I Have Given," "Jokes I Have Laughed

At." Some were almost hilarious in their exactness: "Things I've Yelled at My Brothers." Others I couldn't laugh at: "Things I Have Done in My Anger," "Things I Have Muttered under My Breath at My Parents." I never ceased to be surprised by the contents. Often there were many more cards than I expected. Sometimes fewer than I hoped.

I was overwhelmed by the sheer volume of the life I had lived. Could it be possible that I'd had the time in my twenty years to write each of these thousands or even millions of cards? But each card confirmed this truth. Each was written in my own handwriting. Each signed with my signature.

When I pulled out the file marked "Songs I Have Listened To," I realized the files grew to contain their contents. The cards were packed tightly, and yet after two or three yards, I hadn't found the end of the file. I shut it, shamed, not so much by the quality of music, but more by the vast amount of time I knew that file represented.

When I came to a file marked "Lustful Thoughts," I felt a chill run through my body. I pulled the file out only an inch, not willing to test its size, and drew out a card. I shuddered at its detailed content. I felt sick to think that such a moment had been recorded.

An almost animal rage broke on me. One thought dominated my mind: "No one must ever see these cards! No one must ever see this room! I have to destroy them!" In an insane frenzy I yanked the file out. Its size didn't matter now. I had to empty it and burn the cards. But as I took it at one end and began pounding it on the floor, I could not dislodge a single card. I became desperate and pulled out a card, only to find it as strong as steel when I tried to tear it.

Defeated and utterly helpless, I returned the file to its slot. Leaning my forehead against the wall, I let out a long, self-pitying sigh. And then I saw it. The title bore "People I Have Shared the Gospel With." The handle was brighter than those around it, newer, almost unused. I pulled on its handle and a small box not more than three inches long fell into my hands. I could count the cards it contained on one hand.

And then the tears came. I began to weep. Sobs so deep that they hurt started in my stomach and shook through me. I fell on my knees and cried. I cried out of shame, from the overwhelming shame of it all. The rows of file shelves swirled in my tear-filled eyes. No one must ever, ever know of this room. I must lock it up and hide the key.

But then as I pushed away the tears, I saw Him. No, please not Him. Not here. Oh, anyone but Jesus. I watched helplessly as He began to open the files and read the cards. I couldn't bear to watch His response. And in the moments I could bring myself to look at His face, I saw a sorrow deeper than my own. He seemed to intuitively go to the worst boxes. Why did He have to read every one?

Finally He turned and looked at me from across the room. He looked at me with pity in His eyes. But this was a pity that didn't anger me. I dropped my head, covered my face with my hands and began to cry again. He walked over and put His arm around me. He could have said so many things. But He didn't say a word. He just cried with me.

Then He got up and walked back to the wall of files. Starting at one end of the room, He took out a file and, one by one, began to sign His name over mine on each card!

"No!" I shouted rushing to Him. All I could find to say was "No, no," as I pulled the card from Him. His name shouldn't be on these cards. But there it was, written in red so rich, so dark, so alive. The name of Jesus covered mine. It was written with His blood.

He gently took the card back. He smiled a sad smile and began to sign the cards. I don't think I'll ever understand how He did it so quickly, but the next instant it seemed I heard Him close the last file and walk back to my side. He placed His hand on my shoulder and said, "It is finished."

I stood up, and He led me out of the room. There was no lock on its door. There were still cards to be written.

*If we confess our sins, he is faithful and just and will
forgive us our sins and purify us from all unrighteousness.*

1 JOHN 1:9

Faith Asks

Faith asks:
Who has promised?
Faith looks back:
to mercies given
to promises fulfilled
to victories won
Faith looks forward:
to new songs of deliverance
to new wells of understanding
to new reasons for rejoicing
Faith fills:
the past with gratitude
the present with peace
and the future with hope
Faith finishes:
the course with belief
that what was said in the beginning
has been made perfect in the end.

—SANDY SNAVELY
FROM *CALLED TO REBELLION*

WE'RE SINGING MOTHER INTO PARADISE

HELEN MEDEIROS

I always remember the Twenty-Third Psalm was my parents' favorite Scripture. Every night they would recite it together as they prayed for their eleven children and later many grandchildren and even great grandchildren. After Dad died, Mom continued this tradition. We always knew we were loved and lovingly prayed for. It gave us comfort and even encouragement over the years. Then after Christmas a few years ago, we were called together once again when news came that Mom had another brain aneurysm. Fifteen years ago, she'd had a successful surgery on two other aneurysms, and we had been told there were several more. She could live two weeks or twenty years before another one might burst. So now, at the age of eighty-two, Mom lay in the hospital in Ottawa as the aneurysm began to slowly leak into her brain.

At first, she could communicate with us and indeed even talk and laugh at times, but as the leak grew worse, she became less and less coherent. We prayed with her, sang and read Scriptures softly as she lay there. I had left my husband and four children in Bermuda to be with her, but as the days became weeks and Mom was still with us, I had to say my goodbyes and go home to my family.

Knowing this would probably be the last time I would see my mother,

I said my private farewells to her. By now her brain damage was so severe she could only speak a weak word now and then. Mom could no longer form a clear thought, let alone have any sort of conversation. Indeed, she seemed to be slipping into a coma.

It was a cold snowy day in Ottawa, and I was alone with Mom in that hospital room. I hugged her and thanked her for her wonderful life. I thanked God for everything He had given us in her, and then I opened her Bible and began to read, "The Lord is my shepherd, I shall not want…." I finished the Psalm; she lay still and unresponsive. I then felt led to read it aloud to her again, this time saying, "Mom, the Lord is your shepherd, you shall not want; He makes you lie down in green pastures; He leads you by the still waters, Mom. He restores your soul…." I slowly finished and with tears streaming down my face, I turned and started to leave the room. Before I reached the door, I heard a clear strong voice behind me, and I swung around. Mom was speaking with the voice of a young woman, "The LORD is my shepherd; I shall not want, He makes me to lie down in green pastures; He leads me beside the still waters, He restores my soul." I lifted my hands to praise Almighty God as she spoke every phrase with love, tenderness, and strength, finishing with, "And I will dwell in the house of the LORD forever."

With that last word, she lapsed back into semi-consciousness and never spoke another word. Two days later, the aneurysm burst, and the doctors gave her hours to live…but that mighty woman of God lived for another twelve days as we continued our vigil of thanksgiving, song, and prayer together. Always having been a musical family, we "sang our mother into paradise." As she took her last breath, we softly sang, "She is entering His gates with thanksgiving in her heart; she is entering His courts with praise."

Entering His Gates

Shout for joy to the Lord, all the earth,
Worship the Lord with gladness;
come before him with joyful songs.
Know that the Lord is God.
It is he who made us, and we are his;
we are his people, the sheep of his pasture.
Enter his gates with thanksgiving and his courts with praise;
give thanks to him and praise his name.
For the Lord is good and his love endures forever;
his faithfulness continues through all generations.

PSALM 100

COMING HOME

SHEILA WALSH
FROM *WE BRAKE FOR JOY!*

I love homecomings. That's one of the reasons I treasure every opportunity I have to take a trip back to my native Scotland. On one such trip I was a guest singer at a Billy Graham crusade. I sat with the rain bouncing off the platform as George Beverly Shea sang the lovely hymn,

"Softly and tenderly Jesus is calling, calling for you and for me."

I looked out at the crowd gathered in a Scottish soccer stadium on that soggy Saturday afternoon and marveled that Dr. Billy Graham could fill the place. If it had been Chicago or New York, I would have expected a vast sea of faces, but there, on my own home ground, I was overwhelmed. I watched the crowd hanging on every word.

"Come home, come home
All who are weary come home."

Billy's message was simple and uncompromising. No bells or whistles "wowed" the crowd, just a simple call was made to "Come home." I looked out at shaved heads and tattoos, children running through umbrellas, and I wondered what the response would be.

I wondered if the message sounded too good to be true. I wondered if it sounded too simple.

But then it began… Like a waterfall, people began to stream to the front to receive Christ. I had to bury my face in my hands, overwhelmed with pure joy at being a spectator to such a homecoming. I thought of the Scripture, "I tell you that in the same way there will be more rejoicing in heaven over one sinner who repents than over ninety-nine righteous persons who do not need to repent" (Luke 15:7). I knew a big homecoming celebration was going on in heaven right then.

When the crusade was over, I was waiting at the side of the stage for my ride back to the hotel. A woman wrapped in a plaid raincoat touched my arm. "I enjoyed hearing you sing tonight," she said.

"Thanks!" I replied. "Wasn't it a wonderful evening!"

"It was for me," she said. "I'll never be the same again."

"What do you mean?" I asked.

She stopped and looked at me for a moment as if struggling to put it into words. "I've gone to church all my life, but tonight, I came home."

I put my arms around her and hugged her, and the tears and rain ran rivers down our faces.

WHEN CHRIST COMES

MAX LUCADO
FROM *WHEN CHRIST COMES*

ou are in your car driving home. Thoughts wander to the game you want to see or the meal you want to eat, when suddenly a sound unlike any you've ever heard fills the air. The sound is high above you. A trumpet? A choir? A choir of trumpets? You don't know, but you want to know. So you pull over, get out of your car, and look up. As you do, you see you aren't the only curious one. The roadside has become a parking lot. Car doors are open, and people are staring at the sky. Shoppers are racing out of the grocery store. The Little League baseball game across the street has come to a halt. Players and parents are searching the clouds.

And what they see, and what you see, has never been seen.

As if the sky were a curtain, the drapes of the atmosphere part. A brilliant light spills onto the earth. There are no shadows. None. From whence came the light begins to tumble a river of color—spiking crystals of every hue ever seen and a million more never seen. Riding on the flow is an endless fleet of angels. They pass through the curtains one myriad at a time, until they occupy every square inch of the sky. North. South. East. West. Thousands of silvery wings rise and fall in unison, and over the sound of the trumpets, you can hear the cherubim and seraphim chanting, "Holy, holy, holy."

The final flank of angels is followed by twenty-four silver-bearded elders and a multitude of souls who join the angels in worship. Presently the movement stops and the trumpets are silent, leaving only the triumphant triplet: "Holy, holy, holy." Between each word is a pause. With each word, a profound reverence. You hear your voice join in the chorus. You don't know why you say the words, but you know you must.

Suddenly, the heavens are quiet. All is quiet. The angels turn, you turn, the entire world turns—and there he is. Jesus. Through waves of light you see the silhouetted figure of Christ the King. He is atop a great stallion, and the stallion is atop a billowing cloud. He opens his mouth, and you are surrounded by his declaration: "I am the Alpha and the Omega."

The angels bow their heads. The elders remove their crowns. And before you is a figure so consuming that you know, instantly you know: Nothing else matters. Forget stock markets and school reports. Sales meetings and football games. Nothing is newsworthy. All that mattered, matters no more, for Christ has come....

His Return

For the Lord himself
will come down from heaven,
with a loud command,
with the voice of the archangel
and with the trumpet call of God,
and the dead in Christ will rise first.
After that, we who are still alive
and are left will be caught up together
with them in the clouds to meet the Lord in the air.
And so we will be with the Lord forever.
Therefore encourage each other with these words.

1 THESSALONIANS 4:16-18

Because
I Care

BECAUSE I CARE

Please take a moment to read out loud the verses written on the next page. Although there are hundreds of verses in the Bible that tell about God's love and His gift of salvation, I chose these from the book of Romans in the New Testament.

I care about what happens to you now, but I care even more about where you will spend eternity. If you have never asked Jesus Christ to be your Savior, please consider inviting Him into your life now.

Many years ago I prayed a simple prayer that went something like this:

Dear Jesus,

I believe You are the Son of God and that You gave Your life as a payment for the sins of mankind. I believe You rose from the dead and You are alive today in heaven preparing a place for those who trust in You.

I have not lived my life in a way that honors You. Please forgive me for my sins and come into my life as Savior and Lord. Help me grow in knowledge and obedience to You.

Thank You for forgiving me. Thank You for coming into my life. Thank You for giving me eternal life. Amen.

If you have sincerely asked Jesus Christ to be your Savior, He will never leave you or forsake you. Nothing—absolutely nothing—will be able to separate you from His love.

God bless you, dear one. I'll look forward to meeting you one day in heaven.

—ALICE GRAY

For all have sinned and fall short of the glory of God.
ROMANS 3:23

For the wages of sin is death, but the gift of God
is eternal life in Christ Jesus our Lord.
ROMANS 6:23

But God demonstrates his own love toward us in this:
While we were still sinners, Christ died for us.
ROMANS 5:8

If you confess with your mouth, "Jesus is Lord," and believe
in your heart that God raised him from the dead, you will be saved.
For it is with your heart that you believe and are justified,
and it is with your mouth that you confess and are saved.
ROMANS 10:9–10

Everyone who calls on the name of the Lord will be saved.
ROMANS 10:13

I am convinced that neither death nor life,
neither angels nor demons, neither
the present nor the future,
nor any powers, neither height nor depth
nor anything else in all creation,
will be able to separate us from the love of God
that is in Christ Jesus our Lord.
ROMANS 8:38–39

ACKNOWLEDGMENTS

More than a thousand books and magazines were researched for this collection as well as a review of hundreds of stories sent by friends and readers of the Stories for the Heart collection. A diligent search has been made to trace original ownership, and when necessary, permission to reprint has been obtained. If I have overlooked giving proper credit to anyone, please accept my apologies. If you will contact Multnomah Publishers, Inc., Post Office Box 1720, Sisters, Oregon 97759, correction will be made prior to additional printings. Please provide detailed information.

Notes and acknowledgments are listed by story title in the order they appear in each section of the book. If the author and/or source is unknown, the story is not listed. For permission to reprint any of the stories please request permission from the original source listed below. Grateful acknowledgment is made to authors, publishers, and agents who granted permission for reprinting these stories.

DEDICATION

"Joy in the Morning" by Patti Bisenius. ©1993. Used by permission of the author. Additional words and music available from the author.

COMPASSION

"Lavender Memories" Reprinted from *Heartprints*. © 1999 by Sandra Picklesimer Aldrich and Bobby Valentine. Used by permission of Waterbrook Press, Colorado Springs, CO. All rights reserved.

"Pão, Senhor?" by Max Lucado. Taken from *No Wonder They Call Him the Savior*, © 1986, Multnomah Publishers, Inc., Sisters, OR. Used by permission.

"Something for Stevie" by Dan Anderson

"Meaningful Touch" by Gary Smalley and John Trent, Ph.D. Taken from *Leaving the Light On*, © 1994, Multnomah Publishers, Inc., Sisters OR. Used by permission.

LOVE

1998 by Gold N' Honey Books. Used by permission of Zondervan Publishing House.

"Hope" by Dick Eastman and Jack Hayford from *Living and Praying in Jesus Name,* © 1988. Used by permission of Tyndale House Publishers, Inc. All rights reserved.

"My Grandparent's Game of Love" (originally titled "SHMILY") by Laura Jeanne Allen.©1997. Used by permission of the author.

"The One the Father Loves Most" by Brennan Manning from *Lion and Lamb*, Chosen Books, a division of Baker Book House Company, ©1986.

MAKING A DIFFERENCE

"The Sower" by Alice Gray, © 1999. Used by permission of the author.

"The Most Beautiful Flower" by Cheryl L. Costello-Forshey. © 1998. Cheryl's poetry appears in several *Chicken Soup for the Soul* books. She can be reached at 36240 S. 16th Rd., Barnesville, OH 43713-9504 or call (740) 757-9217 or fax at the same number. Used by permission of the author.

"The Day I Met Daniel" by Richard Ryan. Excerpted from *The Corydon Democrat* magazine, Corydon, IN, July/Aug 1995. Rev. Richard Ryan is an award winning writer and singer, husband and father of three. He is the assistant pastor of Old Capitol United Methodist Church in Corydon, IN. For contact: 141 Heidelberg Rd., West Corydon, IN 47112. Used by permission of the author.

"The Statue" by Dr. Paul Brand and Philip Yancey. Taken from *Fearfully and Wonderfully Made* by Dr. Paul Brand and Philip Yancey. © 1980 by Dr. Paul Brand and Philip Yancey. Used by permission of Zondervan Publishing House.

"Light of the...Storage Closet?" by Max Lucado. Excerpted from *God Came Near*, Multnomah Publishers, Inc., Sisters, OR, © 1987. Used by permission.

"Nurturing across the Generations" by Judy A. Wagner. Used by permission of the author.

"The Quarter That Bought a Pastor" by L. Doward McBain. Condensed from *Leadership Journal*, Summer 1985, © 1983. Used by permission of the author.

"Love That Blossoms" by Nanette Thorsen-Snipes. Excerpted from

CHANGED LIVES

FORGIVENESS

"Mending Fences" by Billy Graham. Excerpted from *The Secrets of Happiness,* © 1985, Word Publishing, Nashville, TN. All rights reserved. Used by permission.

"Lesson in Forgiveness" by Jerry Harpt. © 1997. Used by permission of the author. Jerry Harpt has had a regular newspaper column entitled "Challenging Our Limits" for several years. Many of his inspirational articles have been published in *Chicken Soup for the Soul, Silent Sports Magazine,* and *Woman's World.* He is a recently retired public school teacher and counselor who is now writing full time.

"Seed of Love" by Nanette Thorsen-Snipes. Quoted from *Heart-Stirring Stories of Romance,* compiled by Linda Evans Shepherd, Broadman and Holman Publishers, © 2000. Nanette Thorsen-Snipes has published more than 300 articles, columns, stories, and devotions in more than 35 publications. She may be contacted at P.O. Box 1596, Buford, GA 30515 or jsnipes@aol.com. Used by permission of the author.

"Forgetting" by Luis Palau. Excerpted from *Experiencing God's Forgiveness.* Multnomah Press, © 1984. Used by permission of the author.

"The Waiting Father" by Philip Yancey. Taken from *What's So Amazing About Grace?* By Philip D. Yancey, © 1997 by Philip D. Yancey. Used by permission of Zondervan Publishing House.

"Out of the Carpentry Shop" by Max Lucado. Excerpted from *God Came Near*, Multnomah Publishers, Inc., Sisters, OR, © 1987. Used by permission.

TRUST AND CONTENTMENT

"Kevin's Different World" by Kelly Adkins. Taken from *Campus Life* (Jan/Feb 1999). Used by permission of the author.

"A Brief Blessing" by Gigi Graham Tchividjian. Excerpted from *Currents of the Heart,* Multnomah Publishers, Inc., Sisters, OR, © 1996. Used by permission.

"Yesterday and Tomorrow" by Robert J. Burdette. Cited in *More of...The Best Bits and Pieces,* © 1998, The Economic Press, Inc., Fairfield, NJ 07004, 1-800-526-2554.

"Contrasts" by Joni Eareckson Tada. Excerpted from *Glorious Intruder,* Multnomah Publishers, Inc., Sisters, OR, © 1989. Used by permission.

"Blossoms" by Barbara Baumgardner. Published in *Bereavement*

Magazine, page 44, Nov/Dec 1991. Used by permission of the author.

"Springtime" by Joseph Bayly. Excerpted from *The Last Thing We Talk About,* David C. Cook Publishing, © 1973. Joseph T. Bayly, now deceased, was the author of, among other works, the recently reprinted apocalyptic novel *Winter's Night* (Chariot Victor).

"A Blessing from the Birds" by Gigi Graham Tchividjian. Excerpted from *Currents of the Heart,* Multnomah Publishers, Inc., Sisters, OR, © 1996. Used by permission.

"On the Winning Side" by Charlotte Adelsperger. Used by permission of the author.

"The Kitchen Table" by Philip Gulley. Excerpted from *Front Porch Tales,* Multnomah Publishers, Inc., Sisters, OR, © 1997. Used by permission.

"Now Playing: Sunrise over the Lake" by Ann Campsure, freelance writer, Menasha, WI. © 1999. Used by permission of the author.

"God's in My Basket" by Christopher de Vinck. Taken from *Simple Wonders* by Christopher de Vinck, © 1995 by Christopher de Vinck. Used by permission of Zondervan Publishing House.

"Better Than I Thought" by Ruth Bell Graham. Excerpted from *A Quest for Serenity* by Ruth Bell Graham and G. H. Morling, © 1989, Word Publishing, Nashville, TN. All rights reserved.

"A Baloney Sandwich" by Bob Benson. Excerpted from *See You at the House,* © 1989, Word Publishing, Nashville, TN. All rights reserved.

PRAYER

"Timmy" by Howard Hendricks. Excerpted from *Say It with Love,* Victor Books, Wheaton, IL, © 1973. Used by permission of the author.

"Different Answers" by Nancy Spiegelberg. Excerpted from *Fanfare,* Multnomah Press, Portland, OR, © 1981. Used by permission of the author. Website URL www.godthoughts.com.

"First Prayer" by John Willsea. © 1999. Used by permission of the author.

"Letters to a Stranger" by Susan Morin. Excerpted from *The Christian Reader,* July/August 1999. Used by permission of the author.

"A Small Girl's Prayer" by Helen Roseveare. Excerpted from *Unsolved Miracles,* © 1997, Multnomah Publishers, Inc., Sisters, OR. Used by permission of the author.

"Secret Code" by Sara (Candy) Ann Dubose. Used by permission of the author.

"Nighttime Prayers" by Alice Gray. © 1999. Used by permission of the author.

"Walking by Faith" by Charles R. Swindoll. Taken from *The Strong Family* by Charles R. Swindoll, © 1991 by Charles R. Swindoll. Used by permission of Zondervan Publishing House.

"Crosses" by Patricia Nieland-Collins. Patricia Neiland-Collins is the author of the book *Embers of Life* written under her pen name, Patricia Calvert Neiland. Used by permission of the author.

"A Place of Taking Hold" by Joni Eareckson Tada. Excerpted from *A Quiet Place in a Crazy World*, Multnomah Publishers, Inc., Sisters, OR, © 1993. Used by permission.

FAITH

"Faith Is…" by Pamela Reeve. Excerpted from *Faith Is…*, Multnomah Publishers, Inc., Sisters, OR, © 1994. Used by permission.

"I'm Here" by Robert Strand. Excerpted from *Moments for Mothers*, New Leaf Press, Green Forest, AR, © 1996. Used by permission of the publisher.

"Through" by Billy Graham. Excerpted from *The Secrets of Happiness*, © 1985, Word Publishing, Nashville, TN. All rights reserved.

"The Father's Anguishing Decision" by Carla Muir. Used by permission of the author.

"Her Favorite Verse" by Ron Mehl. Excerpted from *The Cure for a Troubled Heart*, Multnomah Publishers, Inc., Sisters, OR, © 1996. Used by permission.

"Reminder" by Leroy Brownlow. Excerpted from *A Psalm in My Heart*, © 1989, Brownlow Publishing, Fort Worth, TX. Used by permission.

"Doing What Our Father Says" by Luis Palau. Adopted from *Healthy Habits for Spiritual Growth*, by Luis Palau, pp. 84–85, Discovery House Publisher, Grand Rapids, MI, 1994. © 1994, 2000 by Luis Palau.

"Saying Goodbye" by Billy Graham. Excerpted from *Hope for the Troubled Heart*, © 1991, Word Publishing, Nashville, TN. All rights reserved.

"The Shepherd's Psalm" by Robert Strand. Excerpted from *Especially for*

Steps to Peace with God

Step 1   God's Purpose: Peace and Life

God loves you and wants you to experience peace and life—abundant and eternal.

The Bible Says . . .

". . . we have peace with God through our Lord Jesus Christ." Romans 5:1

"For God so loved the world that He gave His only begotten Son, that whoever believes in Him should not perish but have everlasting life." John 3:16

". . . I have come that they may have life, and that they may have it more abundantly." John 10:10b

Since God planned for us to have peace and the abundant life right now, why are most people not having this experience?

Step 2   Our Problem: Separation

God created us in His own image to have an abundant life. He did not make us as robots to automatically love and obey Him, but gave us a will and a freedom of choice.

We chose to disobey God and go our own willful way. We still make this choice today. This results in separation from God.

The Bible Says . . .

"For all have sinned and fall short of the glory of God." Romans 3:23

"For the wages of sin is death, but the gift of God is eternal life in Christ Jesus our Lord." Romans 6:23

Our choice results in separation from God.

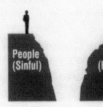

People (Sinful)   God (Holy)

Our Attempts

There is only one remedy for this problem of separation.

Through the ages, individuals have tried in many ways to bridge this gap . . . without success . . .

The Bible Says . . .

"There is a way that seems right to man, but in the end it leads to death." Proverbs 14:12

"But your iniquities have separated you from God; and your sins have hidden His face from you, so that He will not hear." Isaiah 59:2

 ## Step 3 God's Remedy: The Cross

Jesus Christ is the only answer to this problem. He died on the Cross and rose from the grave, paying the penalty for our sin and bridging the gap between God and people.

The Bible Says . . .

". . . God is on one side and all the people on the other side, and Christ Jesus, Himself man, is between them to bring them together . . ." 1 Timothy 2:5

"For Christ also has suffered once for sins, the just for the unjust, that He might bring us to God . . ." 1 Peter 3:18a

"But God demonstrates His own love for us in this: While we were still sinners, Christ died for us." Romans 5:8

God has provided the only way . . . we must make the choice . . .

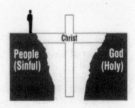

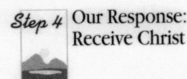

Step 4 | Our Response: Receive Christ

We must trust Jesus Christ and receive Him by personal invitation.

The Bible Says . . .

"Behold, I stand at the door and knock. If anyone hears My voice and opens the door, I will come in to him and dine with him, and he with Me." Revelation 3:20

"But as many as received Him, to them He gave the right to become children of God, even to those who believe in His name." John 1:12

". . . if you confess with your mouth the Lord Jesus and believe in your heart that God has raised Him from the dead, you will be saved." Romans 10:9

Are you here . . . or here?

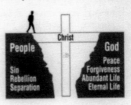

Is there any good reason why you cannot receive Jesus Christ right now?

How to receive Christ:

1. Admit your need (I am a sinner).
2. Be willing to turn from your sins (repent).
3. Believe that Jesus Christ died for you on the Cross and rose from the grave.
4. Through prayer, invite Jesus Christ to come in and control your life through the Holy Spirit. (Receive Him as Lord and Savior.)

What to Pray:

Dear Lord Jesus,

I know that I am a sinner and need Your forgiveness. I believe that You died for my sins. I want to turn from my sins. I now invite You to come into my heart and life. I want to trust and follow You as Lord and Savior.

In Jesus' name. Amen.

_____   _____
Date   Signature

God's Assurance: His Word

If you prayed this prayer,

The Bible Says...

"For 'whoever calls upon the name of the Lord will be saved.'"
Romans 10:13

Did you sincerely ask Jesus Christ to come into your life? Where is He right now? What has He given you?

"For it is by grace you have been saved, through faith—and this is not from yourselves, it is the gift of God—not by works, so that no one can boast." Ephesians 2:8,9

The Bible Says...

"He who has the Son has life; he who does not have the Son of God does not have life. These things I have written to you who believe in the name of the Son of God, that you may know that you have eternal life, and that you may continue to believe in the name of the Son of God." 1 John 5:12–13, NKJV

Receiving Christ, we are born into God's family through the supernatural work of the Holy Spirit who indwells every believer...this is called regeneration or the "new birth."

This is just the beginning of a wonderful new life in Christ. To deepen this relationship you should:

1. Read your Bible every day to know Christ better.
2. Talk to God in prayer every day.
3. Tell others about Christ.
4. Worship, fellowship, and serve with other Christians in a church where Christ is preached.
5. As Christ's representative in a needy world, demonstrate your new life by your love and concern for others.

God bless you as you do.

Billy Graham

If you want further help in the decision you have made, write to:
Billy Graham Evangelistic Association P.O. Box 779, Minneapolis, Minnesota 55440-0779